simply

Chicken

p

This is a Parragon Publishing book
First published in 2001

Parragon Publishing
Queen Street House
4 Queen Street
Bath, BA1 1HE, UK

ISBN: 1-84273-217-X

Printed in China

Produced by The Bridgewater Book Company Ltd.

Art Director: Stephen Knowlden
Editorial Director: Fiona Biggs
Senior Editor: Mark Truman
Editorial Assistant: Tom Kitch
Photography: St John Asprey
Home Economist: Jacqueline Bellefontaine

NOTE
Tablespoons are assumed to be 15 ml.
Unless otherwise stated, milk is assumed
to be whole fat, eggs are medium and pepper
is freshly ground black pepper.

contents

introduction

One of the easiest and least disruptive ways to reduce your fat intake is to change the way you cook. Trying new recipes, even with familiar ingredients, is fun and will result in the pleasure of eating delicious meals that are also healthier.

Chicken has become justly popular around the world and plays an important part in the modern diet, being reasonably priced and nutritionally sound. A versatile meat, it lends itself to an enormous range of cooking methods and cuisines. Its unassertive flavor means that it is equally suited to cooking with both sweet

and savory flavors. Because it has a low fat content, especially without the skin, it is an ideal meat for low cholesterol and calorie-controlled diets. As well as being an excellent source of protein, chicken contains valuable minerals, such as potassium and phosphorus, and some of the B vitamins.

Broiling

Remove any fat from the body cavity. Rinse the bird inside and out with water, then pat dry with paper towels. Season the cavity generously with salt and pepper and add stuffing, herbs, or lemon if wished. Spread the breast of the chicken with softened butter or oil. Set on a rack in a broiling pan or shallow baking dish. Broil the bird, basting two or three times with the pan juices during cooking. If the chicken is browning too quickly, cover it with foil. Use a meat thermometer or insert a skewer into the thickest part of the thigh to see if the meat is done. If the chicken is cooked, the juices will run clear with no trace of pink. Put the bird on a carving board and let rest for 15 minutes before serving. Make a sauce or otherwise a gravy from the juices left in the pan.

Grilling

The intense heat of the grill quickly seals the succulent flesh beneath a crisp, golden exterior. Place the chicken 10–15 cm/4–6 inches away from a moderate heat source. If the chicken seems to be browning too quickly, reduce the heat slightly. If the chicken is grilled at too high a temperature too near to the heat, the outside will burn before the inside is cooked. If it is cooked for too long under a low heat, it will dry out. Divide the chicken into joints to ensure even cooking. Breast meat, if cooked in one piece, can be rather dry, so it is best to cut it into chunks for kabobs. Wings are best for speedy grilling.

Frying

Suitable for small thighs, drumsticks, and joints. Dry the chicken pieces with paper towels so that they brown properly and to prevent spitting during cooking. The chicken can be coated in seasoned flour, egg, and bread crumbs or a batter. Heat oil or a mixture of oil and butter in a deep skillet. When the oil is very hot, add the chicken pieces, skin-side down. Cook until deep golden brown all over, turning the pieces frequently during cooking. Drain well on paper towels before serving.

Sautéing

Ideal for small pieces or small birds such as baby chickens. Heat a little oil or a mixture of oil and butter in a heavy skillet. Add the chicken and fry over a moderate heat until golden brown, turning frequently. Add stock or other liquid, bring to the boil, then cover and reduce the heat. Cook gently until the chicken is cooked through.

Stir-Frying

Good when skinless, boneless chicken is cut into small pieces of equal size to ensure that the meat cooks evenly and stays succulent. Preheat a wok or pan before adding a small amount of oil. When the oil starts to smoke, add the chicken and stir-fry with your chosen flavorings for 3–4 minutes until cooked through. Other ingredients can be cooked at the same time, or the chicken can be cooked by itself, then removed from the pan while you stir-fry the remaining ingredients. Return the chicken to the pan once the other ingredients are cooked.

Casseroling

A good method for cooking joints from larger, more mature chickens, although smaller chickens can be cooked whole. The slow cooking produces tender meat with a good flavor. Brown the chicken in butter or oil or a mixture of both. Add some bouillon, wine, or a mixture of both with seasonings and herbs, cover and cook on top of the stove or in the oven until the chicken is tender. Add a selection of lightly sautéed vegetables about halfway through the cooking time.

Braising

A method which requires little or no liquid. The chicken pieces or a small whole chicken and vegetables are cooked together slowly in a low oven. Heat some oil in an ovenproof, flameproof casserole and gently cook the chicken until golden. Remove the chicken and sauté a selection of vegetables until they are almost tender. Replace the chicken, cover tightly and cook very gently on the top of the stove or in a low oven until the chicken and vegetables are tender.

Poaching

A gentle cooking method that produces tender chicken and a bouillon that can be used to make a sauce to serve with the chicken. Put a whole chicken, a bouquet garni, a leek, a carrot, and an onion in a large flameproof casserole. Cover with water, season, and bring to a boil. Simmer for 1½–2 hours until the chicken is tender. Lift the chicken out, discard the bouquet garni and use the bouillon to make a sauce. Blend the vegetables to thicken the bouillon and serve with the chicken.

Food Safety & Tips

Chicken can become contaminated by salmonella bacteria, which can cause severe food poisoning. When storing, handling, and preparing poultry, certain precautions must be observed to prevent the possibility of food poisoning.

• Check the sell-by date and best before date. After buying, take the chicken home quickly, preferably in a freezer bag or cool box.

• Return frozen birds immediately to the freezer.

• If storing in the refrigerator, remove the wrappings and store any giblets separately. Place the chicken in a shallow dish to catch drips. Cover loosely with foil and store on the bottom shelf of the refrigerator for no more than two or three days, depending on the best before date. Avoid any contact between raw chicken and cooked food during storage and preparation. Wash your hands thoroughly after handling raw chicken.

• Prepare raw chicken on a chopping board that can be easily cleaned and bleached, such as a non-porous, plastic board.

• Frozen birds should be defrosted before cooking. If time permits, defrost for about 36 hours in the refrigerator, or thaw for about 12 hours in a cool place. Bacteria breed in warm food at room temperature and when chicken is thawing. Cooking at high temperatures kills bacteria. There should be no ice crystals and the flesh should feel soft and flexible. Cook the chicken as soon as possible after thawing.

• Make sure that chicken is cooked. Test if the chicken is cooked by using a meat thermometer—the thigh should reach at least 175°F when cooked. Otherwise, pierce the thickest part of a thigh with a skewer—the juices should run clear, not pink or red. Never partially cook chicken with the intention of completing cooking later.

Chicken soup has a long tradition of being comforting and good for us and some cultures even think of it as a cure for all ills. It is certainly satisfying, full of flavor, and easy to digest. For the best results, use a good homemade chicken bouillon, although when time is

at a premium, a good quality bouillon cube can be used instead. Every cuisine in the world has its own favorite version of chicken soup and in this section you'll find a selection of recipes from as far afield as Italy, Scotland, and China.

As chicken is so versatile and quick to cook, it is perfect for innovative and appetizing snacks. Its unassertive flavor means that it can be enlivened by exotic fruits and spices and oriental ingredients, such as mirin, sesame oil, and fresh gingerroot. There are fritters, salads, and drumsticks that are stuffed and baked, or served with delicious fruity salsas. Because chicken pieces travel well and are easy to eat, many of the recipes are ideal to take on picnics or to pack into a lunch box.

soups & appetizers

dickensian chicken broth

This soup is made with traditional Scottish ingredients. Leave for at least two days before being reheated, then served with oatmeal cakes or bread.

Serves 4

⅓ cup pre-soaked dried peas

2 lb diced chicken, fat removed

5 cups chicken bouillon

2½ cups water

¼ cup barley

salt

1 large carrot, peeled and diced

1 small turnip, peeled and diced

1 large leek, thinly sliced

1 red onion, chopped finely

salt and white pepper

1 Put the peas and chicken into a pan, add the bouillon, and water and bring slowly to a boil.

2 Skim the bouillon as it boils using a draining spoon.

3 When all the scum is removed, add the washed barley and salt and simmer for 35 minutes.

4 Add the remaining ingredients and simmer for 2 hours.

5 Skim the surface of the soup again and allow the broth to stand for at least 24 hours. Reheat, adjust the seasoning and serve.

2

3

4

variation

This soup is just as delicious made with beef or lamb. Substitute 8 oz lean beef or lean lamb tenderloin for the chicken. Trim any fat from the meat and cut into thin strips before using.

cook's tip

Use either whole-grain barley or pearl barley. Only the outer husk is removed from whole-grain barley and when cooked it has a nutty flavor and a chewy texture.

chicken consommé

This is a very flavorful soup, especially if you make it from real chicken bouillon. Egg shells are used to give a crystal-clear appearance.

Serves 8-10

8 cups chicken bouillon

⅔ cup medium sherry

4 egg whites plus egg shells

4 oz cooked chicken, sliced thinly

salt and pepper

1 Place the chicken bouillon and sherry in a large pan and heat gently for 5 minutes.

2 Add the egg whites and the egg shells to the chicken bouillon and whisk until the mixture begins to boil.

3 Remove the pan from the heat and allow the mixture to subside for 10 minutes. Repeat this process three times. This allows the egg white to trap the sediments in the chicken bouillon to clarify the soup. Let the consommé cool for 5 minutes.

4 Carefully place a piece of fine cheesecloth over a pan. Ladle the soup over the cheesecloth and strain into the pan.

2

3

4

5 Repeat this process twice, then gently reheat the consommé. Season with salt and pepper to taste and add the cooked chicken slices. Pour the soup into a warm serving dish or individual bowls.

6 Garnish the consommé with any of the suggestions in the Cook's Tip.

cook's tip

Consommé is usually garnished with freshly cooked pasta shapes, noodles, rice, or lightly cooked vegetables. Alternatively, you could garnish it with omelet strips, drained first on paper towels.

tom's chicken soup

The potato has been part of the Irish diet for centuries. This recipe is originally from the north of Ireland, in the beautiful area of Moira, County Down.

Serves 4

3 smoked, streaky, rindless bacon slices, chopped

1 lb 2 oz boneless chicken, chopped

2 tbsp butter

3 medium potatoes, chopped

3 medium onions, chopped

2½ cups giblet or chicken bouillon

2½ cups milk

salt and pepper

⅔ cup heavy cream

2 tbsp chopped fresh parsley

soda bread, to serve

1 Gently dry-fry the bacon and chicken in a large pan for 10 minutes.

2 Add the butter, potatoes, and onions and cook for 15 minutes, stirring all the time.

3 Add the bouillon and milk, then bring the soup to a boil, and simmer for 45 minutes. Season with salt and pepper to taste.

4 Blend in the cream and simmer for 5 minutes. Stir in the chopped fresh parsley, transfer the soup to a warm tureen or individual bowls, and serve with Irish soda bread.

1

2

4

variation

For a more filling, main course soup, you can add any number of different vegetables, for example leeks, celery root, or corn.

cook's tip

Soda bread is not made with yeast as bread usually is. Instead it is made with baking soda as the rising agent. It can be made with all-purpose or whole-wheat flour.

chicken mulligatawny soup

This spicy soup was brought to the west by army and service personnel returning from India. It is very comforting on cold days.

Serves 4

4 tbsp butter

1 onion, sliced

1 garlic clove, finely chopped

1 lb 2 oz chicken, diced

⅓ cup smoked, rindless bacon, diced

1 small turnip, diced

2 carrots, diced

1 small cooking apple, diced

2 tbsp mild curry powder

1 tbsp curry paste

1 tbsp tomato paste

1 tbsp all-purpose flour

5 cups chicken bouillon

salt and pepper

⅔ cup heavy cream

1 tsp chopped fresh cilantro, to garnish

1 Melt the butter in a large pan and cook the onion, garlic, chicken, and bacon for 5 minutes.

2 Add the turnip, carrots, and apple and cook for a further two minutes.

3 Blend in the curry powder, curry paste, and tomato paste and sprinkle over the all-purpose flour.

4 Add the chicken bouillon and bring to a boil, cover, and simmer over a gentle heat for about 1 hour.

5 Liquidize the soup. Reheat, season well with salt and pepper to taste and gradually blend in the heavy cream. Garnish the soup with chopped fresh cilantro and serve over small bowls of boiled or fried rice.

3

4

cook's tip

This soup may be frozen for up to 1 month; if stored for any longer, the spices may cause it to taste musty.

2

chicken & asparagus soup

This light, clear soup has a delicate flavor of asparagus and herbs. Use a good quality bouillon for best results.

1

4

Serves 4

8 oz fresh asparagus

3¾ cups fresh chicken bouillon

⅔ cup dry white wine

1 sprig each fresh parsley, dill, and tarragon

1 garlic clove

⅓ cup vermicelli rice noodles

12 oz lean cooked chicken, finely shredded

salt and white pepper

1 small leek, shredded, to garnish

1 Wash the asparagus and trim away
   the woody ends. Cut each spear
into pieces 1½ inches long.

2 Pour the bouillon and wine into
   a large pan and bring to a boil.

3 Wash the herbs and tie them
   with clean string. Peel the garlic
clove and add to the saucepan with
the herbs, together with the asparagus
and noodles. Cover and simmer for
5 minutes.

3

4 Stir in the chicken and plenty of
   seasoning. Simmer gently for a
further 3–4 minutes until heated through.

5 Trim the leek, slice it down the
   center, and wash under running
water to remove any dirt. Shake dry and
shred finely.

6 Remove the herbs and garlic from
   the pan and discard. Ladle the soup
into warm bowls, sprinkle with shredded
leek and serve at once.

variation

You can use any of your
favorite herbs in this recipe,
but choose those with a subtle
flavor so that they do not
overpower the asparagus.
Small, tender asparagus spears
give the best results and
flavor.

cook's tip

Rice noodles contain no fat
and are an ideal substitute
for egg noodles.

chicken & leek soup

This satisfying soup can be served as a main course. You can add rice and bell peppers to make it even more hearty, as well as colorful.

Serves 6

12 oz boneless chicken

12 oz leeks

2 tbsp butter

5 cups chicken bouillon

1 bouquet garni sachet

salt and white pepper

8 pitted prunes, halved

cooked rice and diced bell peppers
    (optional)

1 Using a sharp knife, cut the chicken and leeks into 1 inch pieces.

2 Melt the butter in a large pan, add the chicken and leeks, and fry for 8 minutes, stirring occasionally.

3 Add the chicken bouillon and bouquet garni sachet to the mixture in the pan, and season with salt and pepper to taste.

5

4 Bring the soup to a boil and simmer over a gentle heat for 45 minutes.

5 Add the pitted prunes with some cooked rice and diced bell peppers (if using), and simmer for 20 minutes. Remove the bouquet garni sachet and discard. Pour the soup into a warm tureen or individual bowls and serve.

2

cooks tip

If you have time, make the chicken bouillon yourself. Alternatively, you can buy good fresh bouillon from stores.

3

variation

Instead of the bouquet garni sachet, you can use a bunch of fresh, mixed herbs, tied together with string. Choose herbs such as parsley, thyme, and rosemary.

cream of chicken soup

Tarragon adds a delicate aniseed flavor to this tasty soup. If you can't find tarragon, use parsley for a fresh taste.

Serves 4

4 tbsp sweet butter

1 large onion, peeled and chopped

10½ oz cooked chicken, shredded finely

2½ cups chicken bouillon

salt and pepper

1 tbsp chopped fresh tarragon

⅔ cup heavy cream

fresh tarragon leaves, to garnish

deep fried croutons, to serve

1

2

1 Melt the butter in a large pan and
sauté the onion for 3 minutes.

2 Add the chicken to the pan with 1¼
cups of the chicken bouillon.

3 Bring to the boil and simmer for
20 minutes. Allow to cool, then
liquidize the soup.

4 Add the remainder of the bouillon
and season with salt and pepper.

5 Add the chopped tarragon, pour the
soup into a tureen or individual
serving bowls, and add a swirl of cream.

6 Garnish the soup with fresh
tarragon and serve with deep fried
croutons.

5

cook's tip

To make garlic croutons, crush
3-4 garlic cloves in a pestle
and mortar and add to the oil.

variation

If you can't find fresh
tarragon, freeze-dried
tarragon makes a good
substitute. Light cream
can be used instead of
the heavy cream.

cream of chicken & tomato soup

This soup is very good made with fresh tomatoes—if you prefer, you can use canned tomatoes, but the flavor won't be as good.

Serves 2

4 tbsp sweet butter

1 large onion, chopped

1 lb 2 oz chicken, shredded very finely

2½ cups chicken bouillon

6 medium tomatoes, chopped finely

pinch of baking soda

salt and pepper

1 tbsp superfine sugar

⅔ cup heavy cream

fresh basil leaves, to garnish

croutons, to serve

1 Melt the butter in a large pan and sauté the onion and shredded chicken for 5 minutes.

2 Add 1¼ cups chicken bouillon to the pan, with the tomatoes and baking soda.

5

2

3 Bring the soup to a boil and simmer for 20 minutes.

4 Allow the soup to cool, then blend in a food processor.

5 Add the remaining chicken bouillon, season with salt and pepper, then add the sugar. Pour the soup into a tureen and add a swirl of heavy cream. Garnish with fresh basil leaves and serve the soup with croutons.

cook's tip

For a healthier version of this soup, use light cream instead of the heavy cream and omit the sugar.

4

variation

For an Italian-style soup, add 1 tbsp chopped fresh basil with the bouillon in step 2. Alternatively, add ½ tsp curry powder or chili powder to make a spicier version of this soup.

chicken soup with cilantro dumplings

Use the strained vegetables and chicken to make little patties. Simply mash with a little butter, shape them into round cakes, and sauté until golden brown.

Serves 6-8

2 lb chicken meat, sliced

½ cup all-purpose flour

½ cup butter

3 tbsp sunflower oil

1 large carrot, chopped

1 stalk celery, chopped

1 onion, chopped

1 small turnip, chopped

½ cup sherry

1 tsp thyme

1 bay leaf

salt and pepper

8 cups chicken bouillon

crusty bread, to serve

DUMPLINGS

½ cup self-rising flour

1 cup fresh bread crumbs

2 tbsp shredded suet

2 tbsp chopped fresh cilantro

2 tbsp finely grated lemon peel

1 egg

salt and pepper

1

5

7

1 Coat the chicken pieces with the flour and season.

2 Melt the butter in a pan and sauté the chicken pieces until they are lightly browned.

3 Add the oil to the pan and brown the vegetables. Add the sherry and the remaining ingredients except the bouillon.

4 Cook for 10 minutes, then add the bouillon. Simmer for 3 hours, strain into a clean pan, and allow to cool.

5 To make the dumplings, mix together all the dry ingredients in a large clean bowl. Add the egg and blend in thoroughly then add enough milk to make a moist dough.

6 Shape into small balls and roll them in a little flour.

7 Cook the dumplings in boiling salted water for 10 minutes.

8 Remove them carefully with a draining spoon and add them to the soup. Cook for 12 minutes, then serve.

cream of chicken & lemon soup

This refreshing soup with its refreshing lemon flavor is perfect on summer days.

Serves 4

4 tbsp butter

8 shallots, sliced thinly

2 medium carrots, sliced thinly

2 celery stalks, sliced thinly

9 oz skinless chicken breast meat,
   chopped finely

3 lemons

5 cups chicken bouillon

salt and pepper

⅔ cup heavy cream

sprigs of parsley and lemon slices, to garnish

variation

For an alternative citrus flavor, use 4 oranges in place of the lemons. The recipe can also be adapted to make duck and orange soup.

1

2

4

1 Melt the butter in a large pan, add the vegetables and chicken, and cook gently for 8 minutes.

2 Thinly pare the lemons and blanch the lemon rind in boiling water for 3 minutes.

3 Squeeze the juice from t he lemons.

4 Add the lemon rind and freshly squeezed lemon juice to the pan with the chicken bouillon.

5 Bring slowly to a boil and simmer for about 50 minutes. Leave the soup to cool then transfer to a food processor and blend until smooth. Return the soup to the pan, reheat, season with salt and pepper to taste, and add the heavy cream. Do not boil at this stage or the soup will curdle.

6 Transfer the soup to a tureen or warm individual bowls. Serve, garnished with parsley and lemon slices.

chicken, guinea fowl & spaghetti soup

Guinea fowl has a similar texture to chicken, and although it has a milder flavor than other game, it has a slightly gamier flavor than chicken.

Serves 6

1 lb 2 oz skinless chicken, chopped

1 lb 2 oz skinless guinea fowl meat

2½ cups chicken bouillon

1 small onion

6 peppercorns

1 tsp cloves

pinch of mace

⅔ cup heavy cream

2 tsp butter

2 tsp all-purpose flour

1 cup quick-cook spaghetti, broken into
　　short pieces and cooked

2 tbsp chopped fresh parsley, to garnish

variation

Instead of spaghetti, use small pasta shapes such as ziti or macaroni.

4

5

6

1 Put the chicken and guinea fowl meat into a large pan with the chicken bouillon.

2 Bring to a boil and add the onion, peppercorns, cloves, and mace. Simmer gently for about 2 hours until the bouillon is reduced by one-third.

3 Strain the soup, skim off any fat, and remove any bones from the chicken and guinea fowl.

4 Return the soup and meat to a clean pan. Add the heavy cream and bring to a boil slowly.

5 To make a roux, melt the butter and stir in the flour until it has a paste-like consistency. Add to the soup, stirring until slightly thickened.

6 Just before serving, add the cooked quick-cook spaghetti.

7 Transfer the soup to individual serving bowls, garnish with parsley and serve.

chinese wonton soup

This Chinese-style soup is delicious as an appetizer to an Asian meal or as a light meal in its own right.

Serves 4-6

FILLING

12 oz ground chicken

1 tbsp soy sauce

1 tsp grated, fresh gingerroot

1 garlic clove, finely chopped

2 tsp sherry

2 scallions, chopped

1 tsp sesame oil

1 egg white

½ tsp cornstarch

½ tsp sugar

about 35 wonton skins

SOUP

6 cups chicken bouillon

1 tbsp light soy sauce

1 scallion, shredded

1 small carrot, cut into
    very thin slices

3

4

6

1 Combine all the ingredients for the filling and mix well.

2 Place a small spoonful of the filling in the center of each wonton skin.

3 Dampen the edges and gather up the wonton skin to form a pouch enclosing the filling.

4 Cook the filled wontons in boiling water for 1 minute or until they float to the top.

5 Remove with a draining spoon. Bring the chicken bouillon to a boil.

6 Add the soy sauce, scallion, carrot, and wontons to the soup. Simmer gently for 2 minutes then serve.

variation

Substitute the chicken for ground pork.

cook's tip

Look for wonton skins in Chinese or Asian stores. Fresh skins can be found in the chilled compartment and they can be frozen if you wish. Wrap in plastic wrap before freezing.

cream of chicken & orange soup

For a tangy flavor, lemons can be used instead of oranges and the recipe can be adapted to make duck and orange soup.

Serves 4

4 tbsp butter

8 shallots, sliced thinly

2 medium carrots, sliced thinly

2 stalks celery, sliced thinly

8 oz skinless chicken breast, chopped finely

3 oranges

5 cups chicken bouillon

salt and white pepper

⅓ cup heavy cream

sprig of parsley and 3 orange slices,
    to garnish

soda bread, to serve

variation

Use 2 small lemons in place of
the oranges. Look for organic
or unwaxed lemons when using
peel.

1 Melt the butter in a large pan, add the shallots, carrot, celery, and chicken meat and cook gently for 8 minutes, stirring occasionally.

2 Using a potato peeler or sharp knife, thinly pare the oranges and blanch the rind in boiling water for about 3 minutes.

3 Squeeze the juice from the oranges. Add the orange rind and orange juice to the pan together with the chicken bouillon.

4 Bring slowly to a boil and simmer for 50 minutes. Cool the soup, then liquidize in a blender or food processor until smooth.

5 Return the soup to the pan, reheat, season to taste, and add the cream. Do not boil at this stage or the soup will curdle.

6 Transfer the soup to a serving dish or individual bowls. Garnish with a sprig of parsley and orange slices and serve with soda bread.

garbanzo bean & chicken soup

This hearty and nourishing soup is an ideal appetizer for a family dinner.

Serves 4

2 tbsp butter

3 scallions, chopped

2 garlic cloves, finely chopped

1 fresh marjoram sprig, finely chopped

5 cups chicken bouillon

12 oz boned chicken breasts, diced

12 oz can garbanzo beans, drained

1 bouquet garni

1 red bell pepper, diced

1 green bell pepper, diced

1 cup small dried pasta shapes, such as
  macaroni

salt and white pepper

croutons, to serve

1

2

4

3 Bring the soup to a boil, lower the heat, and simmer gently for about 2 hours.

4 Add the diced bell peppers and pasta to the pan, then simmer for a further 20 minutes.

5 Transfer the soup to a warm tureen. To serve, ladle the soup into individual serving bowls and serve immediately, garnished with the croutons.

cook's tip

If you prefer, you can use dried garbanzo beans. Cover with cold water and set aside to soak for 5-8 hours. Drain and add the beans to the soup, according to the recipe, and allow an additional 30 minutes-1 hour cooking time.

1 Melt the butter in a large pan. Add the scallions, garlic, fresh marjoram, and the diced chicken, and cook, stirring frequently, over a medium heat for 5 minutes.

2 Add the chicken bouillon, garbanzo beans, and bouquet garni to the pan and season to taste with salt and white pepper.

lemon & chicken soup with spaghetti

This delicately flavored summer soup is surprisingly easy to make.

Serves 4

4 tbsp butter

8 shallots, thinly sliced

2 carrots, thinly sliced

2 celery stalks, thinly sliced

8 oz boned chicken breasts, finely chopped

3 lemons

5 cups chicken bouillon

8 oz dried spaghetti, broken into
   small pieces

salt and white pepper

⅝ cup heavy cream

fresh parsley sprig and

3 lemon slices, halved, to garnish

1 Melt the butter in a large pan. Add the shallots, carrots, celery, and chicken and cook over a low heat, stirring occasionally, for 8 minutes.

2 Thinly pare the lemons and blanch the lemon peel in boiling water for 3 minutes. Squeeze the juice from the lemons.

3 Add the lemon peel and juice to the pan, together with the chicken bouillon. Bring slowly to a boil over a low heat and simmer for 40 minutes.

4 Add the spaghetti to the pan and cook for 15 minutes. Season to taste with salt and white pepper and add the cream. Heat through, but do not allow the soup to boil or it will curdle.

5 Pour the soup into a tureen or individual bowls, garnish with the parsley and half slices of lemon, and serve immediately.

2

cook's tip

You can prepare this soup up to the end of step 3 in advance, so that all you need do before serving is heat it through before adding the pasta and the finishing touches.

1

4

chicken & pea soup

A hearty soup that is so simple to make yet packed with flavor. You can use either whole green peas or green or yellow split peas.

Serves 4-6

3 smoked, streaky, rindless bacon
　　slices, chopped

2 lb chicken, chopped

1 large onion, chopped

1 tbsp butter

2½ cups ready-soaked peas

10 cups chicken bouillon

salt and pepper

⅔ cup heavy cream

2 tbsp chopped fresh parsley

cheesy croûtes, to garnish

1 Put the bacon, chicken, and onion into a large pan with a little butter and cook over a gentle heat for 8 minutes.

2 Add the peas and the bouillon to the pan, bring to a boil, season lightly with salt and pepper, cover and simmer for 2 hours.

3

3 Blend the heavy cream into the soup, sprinkle with parsley, and garnish with cheesy croûtes (see Cook's Tip, left).

1

cook's tip

Croûtes are slices of French bread that are fried or baked, then they can be sprinkled with grated cheese and lightly toasted.

variation

Use 3½ oz chopped ham instead of the bacon, if you prefer.

2

cook's tip

If using dried peas, soak them for several hours or overnight in a large bowl of cold water. Alternatively, bring them to a boil in a pan of cold water. Remove from the heat and leave to cool in the water. Drain and rinse the beans before adding them to the soup.

thai chicken noodle soup

Quick to make, this hot and spicy soup is hearty and warming. If you like your food really fiery, add a chopped dried or fresh chile with its seeds.

1

Serves 4

1 sheet of dried egg noodles
    from a 9 oz pack

1 tbsp oil

4 skinless, boneless chicken thighs,
    diced

1 bunch scallions, sliced

2 garlic cloves, chopped

¾ inch piece fresh ginger root,
    finely chopped

3¾ cups chicken bouillon

scant 1 cup coconut milk

3 tsp red Thai curry paste

3 tbsp peanut butter

2 tbsp light soy sauce

salt and pepper

1 small red bell pepper, chopped

½ cup frozen peas

2

3

1 Put the noodles in a shallow dish and soak in boiling water following the instructions on the packet.

2 Heat the oil in a large saucepan or wok, add the chicken, and fry for 5 minutes, stirring until lightly browned. Add the white part of the scallions, the garlic, and ginger root and sauté for 2 minutes, stirring. Add the bouillon, coconut milk, curry paste, peanut butter, and soy sauce. Season with salt and pepper to taste. Bring to a boil, stirring, then simmer for 8 minutes, stirring

occasionally. Add the red bell pepper, peas, and green scallion tops and cook for 2 minutes.

3 Add the drained noodles and heat through. Spoon into individual bowls and serve with a spoon and fork.

variation

Green Thai curry paste can be used instead of red curry paste for a less fiery flavor.

chicken & corn soup

This heart-warming soup is both quick and easy to make.

Serves 4

1 lb boned chicken breasts, cut into strips

5 cups chicken bouillon

⅝ cup heavy cream

salt and pepper

¾ cup dried vermicelli

1 tbsp cornstarch

3 tbsp milk

6 oz corn kernels

1

4

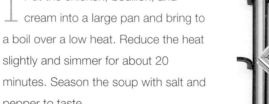

4

cook's tip

If you are short of time, buy ready-cooked chicken, remove any skin, and cut it into slices.

variation

For crab and corn soup, substitute 1 lb cooked crabmeat for the chicken breasts. Flake the crabmeat well before adding it to the pan and reduce the cooking time by 10 minutes. For a Chinese-style soup, substitute egg noodles for the vermicelli and use canned, creamed corn.

1 Put the chicken, bouillon, and cream into a large pan and bring to a boil over a low heat. Reduce the heat slightly and simmer for about 20 minutes. Season the soup with salt and pepper to taste.

2 Meanwhile, cook the vermicelli in lightly salted boiling water for 10–12 minutes, until just tender. Drain the pasta and keep warm.

3 In a small bowl, mix together the cornstarch and milk to make a smooth paste. Stir the cornstarch into the soup until thickened.

4 Add the corn and vermicelli to the pan and heat through.

5 Transfer the soup to a warm tureen or individual soup bowls and serve immediately.

chicken & pasta broth

This satisfying soup makes a good lunch or supper dish and you can use any vegetables that you have at hand. Children will love the tiny pasta shapes.

Serves 6

12 oz boneless chicken breasts

2 tbsp sunflower oil

1 medium onion, diced

1½ cups carrots, diced

9 oz cauliflower flowerets

3¾ cups chicken bouillon

2 tsp dried mixed herbs

4½ oz small pasta shapes

salt and pepper

Parmesan cheese (optional)

Crusty bread, to serve

1

2

3

1 Using a sharp knife, finely dice the chicken, discarding any skin.

2 Heat the oil in a large pan and quickly sauté the chicken and vegetables until they are lightly colored.

3 Stir in the bouillon and herbs. Bring to a boil and add the pasta shapes. Return to a boil, cover, and simmer for 10 minutes, stirring occasionally to prevent the pasta shapes sticking together.

4 Season with salt and pepper to taste and sprinkle with Parmesan cheese, if using. Serve with fresh crusty bread.

cook's tip

You can use any small pasta shapes for this soup—try conchigliette or ditalini or even spaghetti broken up into small pieces. To make a fun soup for children, add animal-shaped or alphabet pasta.

variation

Broccoli flowerets can be used to replace the cauliflower flowerets. Substitute 2 tbsp chopped fresh mixed herbs for the dried mixed herbs.

cheesy garlic drummers

Ideal for informal parties, these tasty chicken drumsticks can be prepared for cooking a day in advance. Instead of baking the chicken drumsticks, you could cook them on the barbecue instead.

Serves 6

1 tbsp butter

1 garlic clove, finely chopped

3 tbsp chopped fresh parsley

½ cup ricotta cheese

4 tbsp grated Parmesan cheese

3 tbsp fresh bread crumbs

salt and pepper

12 chicken drumsticks

lemon slices, to garnish

mixed salad leaves, to serve

variation

Any strongly flavored cheese can be used instead of the Parmesan. Try a mature hard cheese or use another Italian cheese, such as pecorino.

cook's tip

Freshly grated Parmesan has more bite than ready-packed grated Parmesan from stores. Grate only as much as you need and wrap the rest up in foil—it will keep for several months in the refrigerator.

1 Melt the butter in a pan. Add the garlic and sauté gently, stirring, for 1 minute without browning.

2 Remove the pan from the heat and stir in the parsley, the cheeses, bread crumbs, and salt and pepper to taste.

3 Carefully loosen the skin around the drumsticks.

4 Using a teaspoon, push about 1 tablespoon of the stuffing under the skin of each drumstick. Arrange the drumsticks in a large baking pan.

5 Bake in a preheated oven, 375°F, for about 45 minutes. Serve hot or cold, garnished with lemon slices and with mixed salad leaves.

3

4

2

chicken rarebit

A tasty dish that can be served alone as a snack or to accompany a light, clear soup. It is an exciting variation on plain cheese on toast.

Serves 4

2 cups grated crumbly cheese

1⅓ cups shredded, cooked chicken

1 tbsp butter

1 tbsp Worcestershire sauce

1 tsp dry English mustard

2 tsp all-purpose flour

4 tbsp mild beer

salt and pepper

4 slices of bread

1 tbsp chopped fresh parsley, to garnish

cherry tomatoes, to serve

1

3

4

cook's tip

This is a variation of Welsh rarebit, which does not traditionally contain chicken. Welsh rarebit topped with a poached egg is called buck rarebit.

1 Place the grated crumbly cheese, chicken, butter, Worcestershire sauce, mustard, all-purpose flour, and beer in a small pan. Mix all the ingredients together then season with salt and pepper to taste.

2 Gently bring the mixture to a boil and remove from the heat immediately.

3 Using a wooden spoon, beat until the mixture becomes creamy in texture. Allow it to cool.

4 Once the chicken mixture has cooled, toast the bread on both sides and spread with the chicken mixture.

5 Place under a hot broiler until bubbling and golden brown.

6 Garnish with a little chopped parsley and serve with cherry tomatoes.

chicken & herb fritters

These fritters are delicious served with a green salad, a fresh vegetable salsa, or a chili sauce dip.

Makes 8

1 lb 2 oz mashed potato, with butter added

1⅓ cups chopped, cooked chicken

⅔ cups cooked ham, chopped finely

1 tbsp mixed herbs

2 eggs, lightly beaten

salt and pepper

milk

2 cups fresh brown bread crumbs

oil for shallow frying

sprig of fresh parsley, to garnish

mixed salad, to serve

1 In a large bowl, blend the potatoes, chicken, ham, herbs, and 1 egg, and season well.

2 Shape the mixture into small balls or flat pancakes.

3 Add a little milk to the second egg.

4 Place the bread crumbs on a plate. Dip the balls in the egg and milk mixture and roll in the bread crumbs, to coat them completely.

5 Heat the cooking oil in a large skillet and cook the fritters until they are golden brown. Garnish with fresh parsley and serve with a mixed salad.

4

1

2

variation

A mixture of chopped fresh tarragon and parsley makes a fresh and flavorful addition to these fritters.

cook's tip

To make a tomato sauce to serve with the fritters, heat ³/₄ cup sieved tomatoes and 4 tbsp dry white wine. Season, remove from the heat, and add 4 tbsp unsweetened yogurt. Return to the heat and add chili powder to taste.

chicken pepperonata

All the sunshine colors and flavors of the Mediterranean are combined in this easy dish, which would also make a tasty lunch.

Serves 4

8 skinless chicken thighs

2 tbsp whole wheat flour

2 tbsp olive oil

1 small onion, sliced thinly

1 garlic clove, finely chopped

1 each large red, yellow, and green bell
   peppers, sliced thinly

14 oz can chopped tomatoes

1 tbsp chopped oregano

salt and pepper

fresh oregano, to garnish

crusty whole wheat bread, to serve

3

2

1 Remove the skin from the chicken thighs and toss in the flour.

2 Heat the oil in a wide pan and sauté the chicken quickly until sealed and lightly browned, then remove from the pan. Add the onion to the pan and gently sauté until soft. Add the garlic, bell peppers, tomatoes, and oregano, and bring to a boil, stirring.

3 Arrange the chicken over the vegetables, season well with salt and pepper, cover the pan tightly, and simmer for 20–25 minutes or until the chicken is completely cooked and tender.

4 Season to taste, garnish with oregano, and serve with crusty whole wheat bread.

cook's tip

If you do not have fresh oregano, use sieved tomatoes with herbs already added.

variation

For extra flavor, halve the peppers and broil under a preheated broiler until the skins are charred. Leave to cool and remove the skins and seeds. Slice the bell peppers thinly and use in the recipe.

open chicken sandwiches

These tasty sandwiches are good as a snack on their own or they can be served as part of a picnic spread, as they travel well.

3

Serves 6

6 thick slices of bread or a large French
    stick cut lengthways, then cut into
    6 pieces and buttered

3 hard-cooked eggs, the yolk sieved and
    the white chopped

2 tbsp butter, softened

2 tbsp English mustard

1 tsp anchovy extract

pepper

2 cups grated Cheddar cheese

3 cooked, skinless chicken breasts,
    chopped finely

12 slices each of tomato and cucumber

4

5

1 Remove the crusts from the bread
  (optional).

2 Reserve the yolk and the white
  separately from 1 egg.

3 In a large bowl, mix the remaining
  egg with the softened butter,
English mustard, and anchovy extract,
and season well with pepper.

cook's tip

To soften butter, let it
stand at room temperature
for 30 minutes or, if you
are short of time, cream it
in a bowl with a fork.
Alternatively, varieties of
soft butter are now available.

cook's tip

If you prefer a less spicy
flavor, use a milder mustard.
Add mayonnaise if wished and
garnish with watercress.

variation

Add 1³/₄ oz finely chopped
broiled bacon to the chicken
and cheese mixture for a
crunchier texture.

4 Mix in the grated Cheddar cheese
  and chicken and spread the mixture
on the bread.

5 Make alternate rows of the egg yolk
  and the egg white on top of the
chicken mixture. Arrange the tomato
and cucumber slices on top of the egg
and serve.

chicken & cheese jackets

Use the breasts from a roasted chicken for this delicious, healthy snack. Served with a mixed salad, it is an ideal light meal for a summer's day.

Serves 4

4 large baking potatoes

9 oz cooked, boneless chicken breasts

4 scallions

1 cup low-fat soft cheese or Quark

pepper

coleslaw, green salad, or a mixed salad,
    to serve

1 Scrub the potatoes and prick them all over with a fork. Bake in a preheated oven, 400°F, for about 50 minutes until tender, or cook in a microwave on high power for 12–15 minutes.

3

1

2

2 Using a sharp knife, dice the chicken, trim and thickly slice the scallions, and mix with the low-fat soft cheese or Quark.

3 Cut a cross through the top of each potato and pull slightly apart. Spoon the chicken filling into the potatoes and sprinkle with freshly ground black pepper. Serve immediately with coleslaw, green salad, or a mixed salad.

variation

For another delicious filling, sauté 9 oz button mushrooms in a little butter. Mix with the chicken then add $^2/_3$ cup unsweetened yogurt, 1 tbsp tomato paste, and 2 tsp mild curry powder. Blend well and use to fill the jackets.

cook's tip

Look for Quark in the chilled section. It is a low-fat, white, fresh, curd cheese made from cow's milk with a delicate, slightly sour flavor.

oaty chicken pieces

A very low-fat chicken recipe with a refreshingly light, mustard-spiced sauce, which is ideal for a healthy lunchbox or a light meal with salad.

1

Serves 4

⅓ cup rolled oats

1 tbsp chopped fresh rosemary

salt and pepper

4 skinless chicken quarters

1 egg white

½ cup natural low-fat fromage blanc

2 tsp whole grain mustard

grated carrot salad, to serve

variation

To make oaty chicken nuggets, chop up 4 skinless, boneless chicken breasts into small pieces. Reduce the cooking time by about 10 minutes and test if cooked. These nuggets would be ideal at a picnic, buffet, or children's party.

variation

Add 1 tbsp sesame or sunflower seeds to the oat mixture for an even crunchier texture. Experiment with different herbs instead of the rosemary.

2

3

1 Mix together the rolled oats, fresh rosemary, and salt and pepper.

2 Brush each piece of chicken evenly with egg white, then coat in the oat mixture. Place on a baking sheet and bake in a preheated oven, 400°F, for about 40 minutes or until the juices run clear when the chicken is pierced.

3 In a bowl, mix together the fromage blanc and whole grain mustard, season with salt and pepper to taste and serve with the hot or cold chicken with a grated carrot salad.

spicy chicken livers with pak choi

This is a richly flavored dish with a dark, slightly tangy sauce which is popular in China. Take care not to overcook the chicken livers.

Serves 4

12 oz chicken livers

2 tbsp sunflower oil

1 red chile, seeded and finely chopped

1 tsp fresh grated ginger root

2 cloves garlic, finely chopped

2 tbsp tomato ketchup

3 tbsp sherry

3 tbsp soy sauce

1 tsp cornstarch

1 lb pak choi

egg noodles, to serve

1

5

4

1 Using a sharp knife, trim the fat from the chicken livers and slice into small pieces.

2 Heat the oil in a large wok. Add the chicken liver pieces and stir-fry over a high heat for 2–3 minutes.

3 Add the chile, ginger root, and garlic and stir-fry for about 1 minute.

4 Mix together the tomato ketchup, sherry, soy sauce, and cornstarch in a small bowl and set aside.

5 Add the pak choi to the wok and stir-fry until it just wilts.

6 Add the reserved tomato catsup mixture to the wok and cook, stirring to mix, until the juices start to bubble.

7 Transfer to serving bowls and serve hot with noodles.

cook's tip

Fresh ginger root will keep for several weeks in a dry, cool place.

cook's tip

Chicken livers are available fresh or frozen from most supermarkets.

chicken pan bagna

Perfect for a picnic or packed lunch, this Mediterranean-style sandwich can be prepared in advance and wrapped for easy transport.

Serves 6

1 large French stick

1 garlic clove

½ cup olive oil

¾ oz canned anchovy fillets

2 oz cold roast chicken

2 large tomatoes, sliced

8 large, pitted black olives, chopped

pepper

1

2

5

1 Using a sharp bread knife, cut the French stick in half lengthways and open out.

2 Cut the garlic clove in half and rub over the bread.

3 Sprinkle the cut surface of the bread with the olive oil.

4 Drain the anchovies and set aside.

5 Thinly slice the chicken and arrange on top of the bread. Arrange the tomatoes and drained anchovies on top of the chicken.

6 Scatter with the chopped black olives and plenty of black pepper. Sandwich the loaf back together and wrap tightly in foil until required. Cut into slices to serve.

variation

You could use Italian ciabatta or olive-studded focaccia bread instead of the French stick, if you prefer. The last few years have seen a revival of interest in different breads and stores now carry a wide range from home and abroad.

cook's tip

Arrange a few fresh basil leaves in between the tomato slices to add a warm, spicy flavor. Use a good quality olive oil in this recipe for extra flavor.

tuscan chicken livers on toast

Crostini are small pieces of toast with a savoury topping. They are popular in Italy where they are served alongside other antipasto dishes.

Serves 4

2 tbsp olive oil

1 garlic clove, finely chopped

8 oz fresh or frozen chicken livers

2 tbsp white wine

2 tbsp lemon juice

4 fresh sage leaves, finely chopped, or 1 tsp
   dried, crumbled sage

salt and pepper

4 slices ciabatta or other Italian bread

wedges of lemon, to garnish

1 Heat the olive oil in a skillet and
cook the garlic for 1 minute.

2 Rinse and roughly chop the chicken
livers, using a sharp knife.

3 Add the chicken liver to the skillet
together with the white wine and
lemon juice. Cook for 3–4 minutes
or until the juices from the chicken
liver run clear.

4 Stir in the sage and season to taste
with salt and pepper.

5 Under a preheated broiler, toast the
bread for 2 minutes on both sides or
until golden-brown.

6 Spoon the hot chicken livers on top
of the toasted bread and serve
garnished with a wedge of lemon.

3

1

2

variation

Another way to make crostini is to slice a crusty loaf or a French loaf into small rounds or squares. Heat the olive oil in a skillet and sauté the slices of bread until golden brown and crisp on both sides. Remove the crostini from the pan with a draining spoon and leave to drain on paper towels. Top with the chicken livers.

cook's tip

Overcooked liver is dry and tasteless. Cook the chopped liver for only 3-4 minutes—it should be soft and tender.

potted smoked chicken

This recipe can be made a few days ahead and kept chilled until needed. A food processor makes light work of blending the ingredients.

2

5

Serves 4-6

2½ cups chopped smoked chicken

pinch each of grated nutmeg and mace

½ cup butter, softened

2 tbsp port

2 tbsp heavy cream

salt and pepper

sprig of fresh parsley, to garnish

brown bread slices and fresh butter, to serve

4

cook's tip

The Potted Smoked Chicken can be kept in the refrigerator for 2-3 days, but no longer as it does not contain any preservatives. It may be stored in the freezer for a maximum of 1 month.

cook's tip

To make clarified butter: place 1 cup butter in a pan and heat gently, skimming off the foam as the butter heats— the sediment will sink to the bottom of the pan. When the butter has completely melted, remove the pan from the heat and leave to stand for at least 4 minutes. Strain the butter through a piece of cheesecloth into a bowl. Allow the butter to cool a little before spooning it over the surface of the potted chicken.

1 Place the smoked chicken in a large bowl with the remaining ingredients, and season with salt and pepper to taste.

2 Pound until the mixture is very smooth or blend in a food processor.

3 Transfer the mixture to individual earthenware pots or one large pot.

4 Cover each pot with buttered baking parchment and weigh down with cans or weights. Chill in the refrigerator for 4 hours.

5 Remove the parchment and cover with clarified butter (see Cook's Tip).

6 Garnish with a sprig of parsley and serve with slices of buttered brown bread.

old english spicy chicken salad

For this simple, refreshing summer salad you can use leftover roast chicken, or ready-roasted chicken to save time. Add the dressing just before serving, or the spinach will lose its crispness.

Serves 4

9 oz young spinach leaves

3 celery stalks, sliced thinly

½ cucumber

2 scallions

3 tbsp chopped fresh parsley

12 oz boneless, roast chicken, sliced thinly

DRESSING

1 inch piece fresh gingerroot, grated finely

3 tbsp olive oil

1 tbsp white wine vinegar

1 tbsp honey

½ tsp ground cinnamon

salt and pepper

smoked almonds, to garnish (optional)

1 Thoroughly wash the spinach leaves, then pat dry with paper towels.

2 Using a sharp knife, thinly slice the celery, cucumber, and scallions. Toss in a large bowl with the spinach leaves and parsley.

3 Transfer to serving plates and arrange the chicken on top of the salad.

2

4

3

4 In a screw-topped jar, combine all the dressing ingredients and shake well to mix. Season the dressing with salt and pepper to taste, then pour over the salad. Sprinkle with a few smoked almonds, if using.

variation

Substitute corn salad for the spinach, if you prefer.

variation

Fresh young spinach leaves go particularly well with fruit. Try adding a few fresh raspberries or nectarine slices to make an even more refreshing salad.

coronation chicken

This classic salad is good as an appetizer or as part of a buffet. Mango chutney makes a tasty addition.

Serves 6

4 tbsp olive oil

2 lb chicken meat, diced

⅔ cup rindless, smoked bacon, diced

12 shallots

2 garlic cloves, finely chopped

1 tbsp mild curry powder

pepper

1¼ cups mayonnaise

1 tbsp clear honey

1 tbsp chopped fresh parsley

½ cup pitless black grapes, quartered,
   to garnish

cold saffron rice, to serve

1 Heat the oil in a large skillet and add the chicken, bacon, shallots, garlic, and curry powder. Cook slowly for about 15 minutes.

2 Spoon the mixture into a clean mixing bowl.

3 Allow the mixture to cool completely then season with pepper to taste.

cook's tip

You can use this recipe to fill a jacket potato or as a sandwich filling, but cut the chicken into smaller pieces.

4 Blend the mayonnaise with a little honey, then add the chopped fresh parsley. Toss the chicken in the mixture.

5 Place the mixture in a deep serving dish, garnish with the grapes, and serve with cold saffron rice.

1

4

4

variation

Add 2 tbsp chopped fresh apricots and 2 tbsp slivered almonds to the sauce in step 4. For a healthier version of this dish, replace the mayonnaise with the same quantity of unsweetened yogurt and omit the honey, otherwise the sauce will be too runny.

waldorf summer chicken salad

This colorful and healthy dish is a variation of a classic salad. Served with crusty brown rolls, it is an ideal light meal for a summer's day.

Serves 4

1 lb 2 oz red dessert apples, diced

3 tbsp fresh lemon juice

⅔ cup light mayonnaise

1 head of celery

4 shallots, sliced

1 garlic clove, finely chopped

¾ cup walnuts, chopped

1 lb 2 oz cooked chicken, cubed

1 Cos lettuce

pepper

sliced apple and walnuts, to garnish

cook's tip

Soaking the apples in lemon juice prevents discoloration.

variation

Instead of the shallots, use scallions for a milder flavor. Trim the scallions and slice finely.

1

2

4

3 Add the celery, shallots, garlic, and walnuts to the apple and mix together.

4 Stir in the mayonnaise and blend thoroughly.

5 Add the cooked chicken to the bowl and mix well.

6 Line a glass salad bowl or serving dish with the lettuce leaves. Pile the chicken salad into the center, sprinkle with pepper, and garnish with the apple slices and walnuts.

1 Place the apples in a bowl with the lemon juice and 1 tablespoon of mayonnaise. Leave for 40 minutes.

2 Using a sharp knife, slice the celery very thinly.

solomongundy

This recipe is ideally suited as a cold platter for a buffet party or a spectacular starter for a special meal.

Serves 4

1 large lettuce

4 chicken breasts,
   cooked and sliced thinly

8 rollmop herrings and
   their marinade

6 hard-cooked eggs, quartered

⅔ cup cooked ham, sliced

2⅔ cups roast beef, sliced

⅔ cup roast lamb, sliced

1 cup snow peas, cooked

¾ cup pitless black grapes,

20 stuffed olives, sliced

12 shallots, boiled

½ cup slivered almonds

⅓ cup golden raisins

2 oranges

sprig of mint

salt and pepper

fresh crusty bread, to serve

1 Spread out the lettuce leaves on a large oval platter.

2 Arrange the chicken in three sections on the platter.

3 Place the rollmops, eggs, and meats in lines or sections over the remainder of the platter.

4 Use the snow peas, grapes, olives, shallots, almonds, and golden raisins to fill in the spaces between the sections.

5 Grate the peel from the oranges and sprinkle over the whole platter. Peel and slice the oranges and add the orange slices and mint sprig to the platter. Season well with salt and pepper. Sprinkle with the herring marinade and serve with fresh crusty bread.

variation

Should you wish, serve with cold, cooked vegetables, such as sliced beans, baby corn, and cooked beet.

2

1

3

suprême of chicken with pears & blue cheese

The sweetness of the pears complements perfectly the sharp taste of the blue cheese in this delicious warm salad.

Serves 6

¼ cup olive oil

6 shallots, sliced

1 garlic clove, finely chopped

2 tbsp chopped fresh tarragon

1 tbsp English mustard

salt and pepper

6 skinless, boneless chicken breasts

1 tbsp flour

⅔ cup chicken bouillon

1 dessert apple, diced finely

1 tbsp chopped walnuts

2 tbsp heavy cream

SALAD

3½ cups cooked rice

2 large pears, diced

1 cup blue cheese, diced

1 red bell pepper, diced

1 tbsp chopped fresh cilantro

1 tbsp sesame oil

1

2

4

1 Place the olive oil, shallots, garlic, tarragon, and mustard in a deep bowl. Season well and mix the ingredients together thoroughly.

2 Place the chicken in the marinade to coat completely, cover with plastic wrap and chill in the refrigerator for about 4 hours.

3 Drain the chicken, reserving the marinade. Quickly cook the chicken in a large, deep non-stick skillet for 4 minutes on each side. Transfer the chicken to a warm serving dish.

4 Add the marinade to the pan, bring to a boil, and sprinkle with the flour. Add the chicken bouillon, apple, and walnuts and gently simmer for 5 minutes. Return the chicken to the sauce, add the heavy cream, and cook for 2 minutes.

5 Mix the salad ingredients together, place a little on each plate, and top with a chicken breast and a spoonful of the sauce.

One of the marvelous qualities of chicken
is that when it is cut into small pieces,
it can be cooked very quickly, which is
welcome for those of us who are too busy
to spend a lot of time preparing meals. In
this section, you can select a
tasty nutritious dish that won't take hours

to make. Pasta makes a perfect partner for
chicken as it is also quick to cook—Italian
Chicken Spirals look impressive and will
fool guests into thinking that you have
spent hours slaving away in the kitchen.
Chicken breasts are cooked with a delicious basil,
filbert, and garlic filling and then served on a bed
of pasta, olives, and sun-dried tomatoes. Smaller
cuts of chicken are also ideal for stir-fries that
can be quickly cooked to produce tender, moist, and
flavorful chicken. Speedy Peanut Pan-Fry is a crunchy

stir-fry that is served with noodles.
Risottos are also an excellent choice for
when you are in a hurry—this chapter
contains two risotto recipes although the
variations for risotto are endless.

quick
dishes

chicken chop suey

Both well-known and popular, chop suey dishes are easy to make and delicious. They are based on beansprouts and soy sauce with meat or vegetable flavoring.

Serves 4

4 tbsp light soy sauce

2 tsp light brown sugar

1¼ lb skinless, boneless chicken breasts

3 tbsp vegetable oil

2 onions, quartered

2 garlic cloves, finely chopped

12 oz beansprouts

3 tsp sesame oil

1 tbsp cornstarch

3 tbsp water

2 cups chicken bouillon

shredded leek, to garnish

1 Mix the soy sauce and sugar together, stirring until the sugar has dissolved.

2 Trim any fat from the chicken and cut the meat into thin strips. Place the chicken strips in a shallow glass dish and spoon the soy mixture over them, turning to coat. Leave to marinate in the refrigerator for 20 minutes.

3 Heat the oil in a preheated wok. Add the chicken and stir-fry for 2–3 minutes, until golden brown.

4 Add the onions and garlic and cook for a further 2 minutes. Add the beansprouts, cook for a further 4–5 minutes, then add the sesame oil.

5 Blend the cornstarch with the water to form a smooth paste. Pour the bouillon into the wok, together with the cornflour paste, and bring to a boil, stirring constantly until the sauce is thickened and clear. Transfer to a warm serving dish, garnish with shredded leek, and serve immediately.

variation

This recipe may be made with strips of lean steak, pork, or with mixed vegetables. Change the type of bouillon accordingly.

2

3

4

chicken with cumin seeds & eggplant

This is a delicious curried chicken and eggplant dish, flavored with tomatoes and seasoned with fresh mint.

Serves 4

5 tbsp sunflower oil

2 cloves garlic, finely chopped

1 tbsp cumin seeds

1 tbsp mild curry powder

1 tbsp paprika

1 lb boneless, skinless chicken breasts

1 large eggplant, cubed

4 tomatoes, cut into quarters

⅓ cup chicken bouillon

1 tbsp fresh lemon juice

½ tsp salt

⅔ cup unsweetened yogurt

1 tbsp chopped fresh mint

1 Heat 2 tablespoons of the sunflower oil in a large preheated wok.

2 Add the garlic, cumin seeds, curry powder, and paprika to the wok and stir-fry for 1 minute.

3 Using a sharp knife, thinly slice the chicken breasts.

4 Add the rest of the oil to the wok and stir-fry the chicken for 5 minutes.

5 Add the eggplant cubes, tomatoes, and chicken bouillon and bring to a boil. Reduce the heat and leave to simmer for about 20 minutes.

6 Stir in the lemon juice, salt, and yogurt and cook over a gentle heat for a further 5 minutes, stirring occasionally.

7 Scatter with chopped fresh mint and transfer to serving bowls. Serve immediately.

cook's tip

Once the yogurt has been added, do not boil the sauce as it will curdle.

chicken, spring green & yellow bean stir-fry

Yellow bean sauce is made from yellow soy beans and is available in most stores. Try to buy a chunky sauce rather than a smooth sauce for texture.

3

Serves 4

2 tbsp sunflower oil

1 lb skinless, boneless chicken breasts

2 cloves garlic, finely chopped

1 green bell pepper

1½ cups snow peas

6 scallions, sliced, plus extra to garnish

8 oz spring greens or cabbage, shredded

5¾ oz jar yellow bean sauce

3 tbsp roasted cashew nuts

4

5

cook's tip

Do not add salted cashew nuts to this dish, otherwise when combined with the slightly salty sauce, the dish will be very salty indeed.

1 Heat the sunflower oil in a large preheated wok.

2 Using a sharp knife, slice the chicken into thin strips.

3 Add the chicken to the wok together with the garlic. Stir-fry for about 5 minutes or until the chicken is sealed on all sides and beginning to turn golden.

4 Using a sharp knife, seed the green bell pepper and cut into thin strips.

5 Add the snow peas, scallions, green bell pepper strips, and spring

greens or cabbage to the wok. Stir-fry for a further 5 minutes or until the vegetables are just tender.

6 Stir in the yellow bean sauce and heat through for about 2 minutes or until the mixture starts to bubble.

7 Scatter with the roasted cashew nuts.

8 Transfer the chicken, spring green, and yellow bean stir-fry to warm serving plates and garnish with extra scallions, if desired. Serve the stir-fry immediately.

peppered chicken with sugar snap peas

Crushed mixed peppercorns coat tender, thin strips of chicken which are cooked with green and red bell peppers for a really colorful dish.

Serves 4

2 tbsp tomato catsup

2 tbsp soy sauce

1 lb boneless, skinless chicken breasts

2 tbsp mixed peppercorns, ground

2 tbsp sunflower oil

1 red bell pepper

1 green bell pepper

2½ cups sugar snap peas

2 tbsp oyster sauce

variation

Use snow peas instead of sugar snap peas, if you prefer.

1

2

1 Mix the tomato catsup with the soy sauce in a bowl.

2 Using a sharp knife, slice the chicken into thin strips. Toss the chicken in the tomato catsup and soy sauce mixture.

3 Sprinkle the ground peppercorns on to a plate. Dip the coated chicken in the peppercorns until evenly coated.

4 Heat the sunflower oil in a preheated wok.

5 Add the chicken to the wok and stir-fry for 5 minutes.

6 Seed and slice the bell peppers.

7 Add the bell peppers to the wok together with the sugar snap peas and stir-fry for a further 5 minutes.

8 Add the oyster sauce and allow to bubble for 2 minutes. Transfer to serving bowls and serve immediately.

6

stir-fried ginger chicken

The oranges add color and piquancy to this refreshing dish, which complements the chicken well. It needs only simple accompaniments.

Serves 4

2 tbsp sunflower oil

1 onion, sliced

6 oz carrots, cut into thin sticks

1 clove garlic, finely chopped

12 oz boneless skinless chicken breasts

2 tbsp fresh gingerroot, peeled and grated

1 tsp ground ginger

4 tbsp sweet sherry

1 tbsp tomato paste

1 tbsp demerara sugar

⅓ cup orange juice

1 tsp cornstarch

1 orange, peeled and segmented

fresh snipped chives, to garnish

cook's tip

Make sure that you do not continue cooking the dish once the orange segments have been added in step 4, otherwise they will break up.

1

2

3

1 Heat the oil in a large preheated wok. Add the onion, carrots, and garlic, and stir-fry over a high heat for 3 minutes or until the vegetables begin to soften.

2 Using a sharp knife, slice the chicken into thin strips. Add the chicken to the wok together with the fresh gingerroot and ground ginger. Stir-fry for a further 10 minutes, or until the chicken is well cooked through and golden in color.

3 Mix together the sherry, tomato paste, sugar, orange juice, and cornstarch in a bowl. Stir the mixture into the wok and heat through until the mixture bubbles and the juices start to thicken.

4 Add the orange segments and carefully toss to mix.

5 Transfer the stir-fried chicken to warm serving bowls and garnish with freshly snipped chives. Serve immediately.

honey & soy stir-fried chicken

Honey is often added to Chinese recipes for sweetness. It combines well with the saltiness of the soy sauce.

Serves 4

2 tbsp honey

3 tbsp light soy sauce

1 tsp Chinese five-spice powder

1 tbsp sweet sherry

1 clove garlic, finely chopped

8 chicken thighs

1 tbsp sunflower oil

1 red chili

1¼ cups baby corn, halved

8 scallions, sliced

1½ cups beansprouts

1 Mix together the honey, soy sauce, Chinese five-spice powder, sherry, and garlic in a large bowl.

2 Using a sharp knife, make 3 slashes in the skin of each chicken thigh. Brush the honey and soy marinade over the chicken thighs, cover and leave to stand for at least 30 minutes.

3 Heat the oil in a large preheated wok.

4 Add the chicken to the wok and cook over a fairly high heat for 12–15 minutes, or until the chicken browns and the skin begins to crisp. Remove the chicken with a draining spoon.

5 Using a sharp knife, seed and very finely chop the chili.

6 Add the chili, corn, scallions, and beansprouts to the wok and stir-fry for 5 minutes.

7 Return the chicken to the wok and mix all of the ingredients together until completely heated through. Serve immediately.

cook's tip

Chinese five-spice powder is found in most large stores and is a blend of aromatic spices.

1

2

5

cashew chicken in yellow bean sauce

Chicken and cashew nuts are a great classic combination, and this recipe is no exception. Flavored with yellow bean sauce, it is a quick and delicious dish.

Serves 4

1 lb boneless chicken breasts

2 tbsp vegetable oil

1 red onion, sliced

1½ cups flat mushrooms, sliced

⅓ cup cashew nuts

2¾ oz jar yellow bean sauce

fresh cilantro, to garnish

egg fried rice or plain boiled rice, to serve

1

3

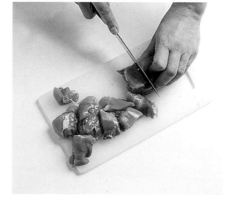

4

1 Using a sharp knife, remove the excess skin from the chicken breasts if desired. Cut the chicken into small, bite-sized chunks.

2 Heat the vegetable oil in a preheated wok.

3 Add the chicken to the wok and stir-fry for 5 minutes.

4 Add the red onion and mushrooms to the wok and continue to stir-fry for a further 5 minutes.

5 Place the cashew nuts on a cookie sheet and toast under a preheated medium broiler until just browning–this brings out their flavor.

6 Toss the toasted cashew nuts into the wok together with the yellow bean sauce. Allow the sauce to bubble for 2–3 minutes.

7 Transfer to warm serving bowls and garnish with fresh cilantro. Serve hot with egg fried rice or plain boiled rice.

cook's tip

Chicken thighs could be used instead of the chicken breasts for a more economical dish.

chicken with cumin seeds & bell peppers

Cumin seeds are more frequently associated with Indian cooking, but they are used in this Chinese recipe for their earthy flavor. You could use ½ teaspoon of ground cumin instead.

Serves 4

1 lb boneless, skinless chicken breasts

2 tbsp sunflower oil

1 clove garlic, finely chopped

1 tbsp cumin seeds

1 tbsp grated fresh ginger root

1 red chile, seeded and sliced

1 red bell pepper, seeded and sliced

1 green bell pepper, seeded and sliced

1 yellow bell pepper, seeded and sliced

1 cup beansprouts

12 oz pak choi or other green leaves

2 tbsp sweet chili sauce

3 tbsp light soy sauce

deep-fried crispy ginger, to garnish
(see Cook's Tip)

1 Using a sharp knife, slice the chicken breasts into thin strips.

2 Heat the oil in a large preheated wok.

3 Add the chicken to the wok and stir–fry for 5 minutes.

4 Add the garlic, cumin seeds, ginger root, and chile to the wok, stirring to mix.

5 Add all of the bell peppers to the wok and stir-fry for a further 5 minutes.

6 Toss in the beansprouts and pak choi together with the sweet chili sauce and soy sauce and continue to cook until the pak choi leaves start to wilt.

6

7 Transfer to warm serving bowls and garnish with deep-fried ginger root (see Cook's Tip).

4

5

cook's tip

To make the deep-fried ginger root garnish, peel, and thinly slice a large piece of ginger root, using a sharp knife. Carefully lower the slices into a wok or small pan of hot oil and cook for about 30 seconds. Remove the deep-fried ginger root with a draining spoon, transfer to sheets of paper towels and leave to drain thoroughly.

sweet & sour chicken with mango

This is quite a sweet dish as mango has a sweet, scented flavor.

Serves 4

1 tbsp sunflower oil

6 skinless, boneless chicken thighs

1 ripe mango

2 cloves garlic, finely chopped

8 oz leeks, shredded

1 cup beansprouts

⅔ cup mango juice

1 tbsp white wine vinegar

2 tbsp honey

2 tbsp tomato catsup

1 tsp cornstarch

cook's tip

Mango juice is available in jars from most supermarkets and is quite thick and sweet. If unavailable, Mash and sieve a ripe mango and add a little water to make up the required quantity.

2

4

1 Heat the sunflower oil in a large preheated wok.

2 Using a sharp knife, cut the chicken into bite-sized cubes.

3 Add the chicken to the wok and stir-fry over a high heat for 10 minutes, tossing frequently until the chicken is cooked through and golden in color.

4 Meanwhile, peel and slice the mango.

5 Add the garlic, leeks, mango, and beansprouts to the wok and stir-fry for a further 2–3 minutes, or until softened.

6 Mix together the mango juice, white wine vinegar, honey, and tomato catsup with the cornstarch in a measuring pitcher.

7 Pour the mango juice and cornstarch mixture into the wok and stir-fry for a further 2 minutes, or until the juices start to thicken.

8 Transfer to a warmed serving dish and serve immediately.

6

thai red chicken with cherry tomatoes

This is a really colorful dish, the red of the tomatoes perfectly complementing the orange sweet potato.

Serves 4

1 tbsp sunflower oil

1 lb boneless, skinless chicken

2 cloves garlic, finely chopped

2 tbsp Thai red curry paste

2 tbsp fresh grated galangal or gingerroot

1 tbsp tamarind paste

4 lime leaves

8 oz sweet potato

2½ cups coconut milk

8 oz cherry tomatoes, halved

3 tbsp chopped fresh cilantro

cooked jasmine or Thai fragrant rice, to serve

1 Heat the sunflower oil in a large preheated wok.

2 Thinly slice the chicken. Add the chicken to the wok and stir-fry for 5 minutes.

3 Add the garlic, curry paste, galangal or gingerroot, tamarind, and lime leaves to the wok and stir-fry for 1 minute.

4 Using a sharp knife, peel and dice the sweet potato.

5 Add the coconut milk and sweet potato to the mixture in the wok and bring to a boil. Allow to bubble over

3

4

a medium heat for 20 minutes, or until the juices start to thicken and reduce.

6 Add the cherry tomatoes and cilantro to the curry and cook for a further 5 minutes, stirring occasionally. Transfer to serving plates and serve hot with cooked jasmine or Thai fragrant rice.

5

cook's tip

Galangal is a spice very similar to ginger and is used to replace the latter in Thai cuisine. It can be bought fresh from Asian food stores but is also available dried and as a powder. The fresh root, which is not as pungent as ginger, needs to be peeled before slicing to use.

stir-fried chicken with lemon & sesame

Sesame seeds have a strong flavor which adds nuttiness to recipes. They are perfect for coating these thin chicken strips.

Serves 4

4 boneless, skinless chicken breasts

1 egg white

2 tbsp sesame seeds

2 tbsp vegetable oil

1 onion, sliced

1 tbsp demerara sugar

finely grated peel and juice of 1 lemon

3 tbsp lemon curd

7 oz can waterchestnuts

lemon peel, to garnish

1 Place the chicken breasts between 2 sheets of plastic wrap and pound with a rolling pin to flatten. Slice the chicken into thin strips.

2 Whisk the egg white until light and foamy.

3 Dip the chicken strips into the egg white, then into the sesame seeds until coated evenly.

1

4 Heat the oil in a large preheated wok.

5 Add the onion to the wok and stir-fry for 2 minutes or until just softened.

6 Add the sesame-coated chicken to the wok and continue stir-frying for 5 minutes, or until golden.

7 Mix together the sugar, lemon peel, lemon juice, and the lemon curd and add the mixture to the wok. Allow the lemon mixture to bubble slightly without stirring.

8 Drain the waterchestnuts and slice them thinly, using a sharp knife. Add the waterchestnuts to the wok and heat through for 2 minutes. Transfer to serving bowls, garnish with lemon peel, and serve hot.

cook's tip

Waterchestnuts are commonly added to Chinese recipes for their crunchy texture as they do not have a great deal of flavor.

3

8

chicken, bell pepper, & orange stir-fry

Chicken thighs are inexpensive, meaty portions of the chicken which are readily available. The meat is not as tender as the breast but it is perfect for stir-frying.

Serves 4

3 tbsp sunflower oil

12 oz boneless chicken thighs, skinned and
    cut into thin strips

1 onion, sliced

1 clove garlic, finely chopped

1 red bell pepper, seeded and sliced

1¼ cups snow peas

4 tbsp light soy sauce

4 tbsp sherry

1 tbsp tomato paste

finely grated peel and juice of 1 orange

1 tsp cornstarch

2 oranges

1 cup beansprouts

cooked rice or noodles, to serve

cook's tip

Beansprouts are sprouting mung
beans and are a regular
ingredient in Chinese cooking.
They require very little
cooking and may even be eaten
raw, if wished.

2

1 Heat the sunflower oil in a large
preheated wok.

2 Add the strips of chicken to the wok
and stir-fry for 2–3 minutes or until
sealed on all sides.

3 Add the sliced onion, garlic, bell
pepper, and snow peas to the wok.
Stir-fry the mixture for a further 5
minutes, or until the vegetables are just
becoming tender and the chicken is
completely cooked through.

4 Mix together the soy sauce, sherry,
tomato paste, orange peel and
juice, and the cornstarch in a measuring
pitcher.

5 Add the mixture to the wok and
cook, stirring, until the juices start
to thicken.

6 Using a sharp knife, peel and
segment the oranges.

7 Add the orange segments and
beansprouts to the mixture in the
wok and heat through for a further
2 minutes.

8 Transfer the stir-fry to serving plates
and serve at once with cooked rice
or noodles.

4

6

chicken, corn, & snow pea stir-fry

This quick and healthy dish is stir-fried, which means you need use only the minimum of fat. If you don't have a wok, use a wide skillet instead.

1

Serves 4

4 skinless, boneless chicken breasts

1⅓ cups baby corn

9 oz snow peas

2 tbsp sunflower oil

1 tbsp sherry vinegar

1 tbsp honey

1 tbsp light soy sauce

1 tbsp sunflower seeds

pepper

rice or egg noodles, to serve

3

4

1 Using a sharp knife, slice the chicken breasts into long, thin strips. Cut the baby corn in half lengthways and top and tail the snow peas. Set the vegetables aside until required.

2 Heat the sunflower oil in a wok or a wide skillet and sauté the chicken over a fairly high heat, stirring constantly, for 1 minute.

3 Add the corn and snow peas and stir over a medium heat for 5–8 minutes, until evenly cooked.

4 Mix together the sherry vinegar, honey, and soy sauce and stir into the pan with the sunflower seeds. Season with pepper to taste. Cook, stirring constantly, for 1 minute. Serve the sauté hot with rice or Chinese egg noodles.

cook's tip

Rice vinegar or balsamic vinegar makes a good substitute for the sherry vinegar.

stir-fried garlic chicken with cilantro & lime

Garlic and cilantro butter flavors and moistens chicken breasts which are served with a caramelized sauce, sharpened with lime juice.

Serves 4

4 large skinless, boneless chicken breasts

3 tbsp garlic butter, softened

3 tbsp chopped fresh cilantro, plus extra
    to garnish (optional)

1 tbsp sunflower oil

finely grated peel and juice of 2 limes

4 tbsp palm sugar or demerara sugar

boiled rice, to serve

cook's tip

Be sure to check that the chicken is cooked through before slicing and serving. Cook over a gentle heat so as not to overcook the outside, while leaving the inside raw.

1 Place each chicken breast between 2 sheets of plastic wrap and pound with a rolling pin until flattened to ½ inch thick.

2 Mix together the garlic butter and cilantro and spread over each flattened chicken breast. Roll up and secure with a toothpick.

3

2

2

3 Heat the oil in a wok. Add the chicken rolls and cook, turning, for 15–20 minutes or until cooked through.

4 Remove the chicken from the wok and transfer to a board. Cut each chicken roll into slices.

5 Add the lime peel, juice, and sugar to the wok and heat gently, stirring, until the sugar has dissolved. Raise the heat and allow to bubble for 2 minutes.

6 Arrange the chicken on warmed serving plates and spoon the pan juices over to serve.

7 Garnish with extra cilantro if desired, and serve with boiled rice.

speedy peanut pan-fry

A complete main course cooked within ten minutes. Thread egg noodles are the ideal accompaniment because they can be cooked quickly and easily while the stir-fry sizzles.

Serves 4

2 cups zucchini

1⅓ cups baby corn

3¾ cups white mushrooms

3 cups thread egg noodles

2 tbsp corn oil

1 tbsp sesame oil

8 boneless chicken thighs

  or 4 breasts, sliced thinly

1½ cups beansprouts

4 tbsp smooth peanut butter

2 tbsp soy sauce

2 tbsp lime or lemon juice

pepper

½ cup roasted peanuts

sprig of cilantro, to garnish

1

3

1 Using a sharp knife, trim and thinly slice the zucchini, corn, and white mushrooms.

2 Bring a large pan of lightly salted boiling water to a boil and cook the noodles for 3–4 minutes. Meanwhile, heat the corn oil and sesame oil in a large skillet or wok and sauté the chicken over a high heat for 1 minute.

3 Add the sliced zucchini, corn, and white mushrooms and stir-fry for 5 minutes.

4

4 Add the beansprouts, peanut butter, soy sauce, lime or lemon juice, and pepper, then cook for a further 2 minutes.

5 Drain the noodles, transfer to a serving dish, and scatter with the peanuts. Serve with the stir-fried chicken and vegetables, garnished with a sprig of cilantro.

cook's tip

Try serving this stir-fry with rice sticks. These are broad, pale, translucent ribbon noodles made from ground rice.

coconut chicken curry

Okra or ladies, fingers are slightly bitter in flavor. The pineapple and coconut in this recipe offsets them in both color and flavor.

Serves 4

2 tbsp sunflower oil or 1 oz ghee

1 lb boneless, skinless chicken thighs
   or breasts

1 cup okra

1 large onion, sliced

2 cloves garlic, finely chopped

3 tbsp mild curry paste

2¼ cups chicken bouillon

1 tbsp fresh lemon juice

½ cup creamed coconut

1¼ cups fresh or canned pineapple, cubed

⅔ cup thick, unsweetened yogurt

2 tbsp chopped fresh cilantro

freshly boiled rice, to serve

lemon wedges and fresh cilantro sprigs,
   to garnish

1 Heat the sunflower oil or ghee in a large preheated wok.

2 Using a sharp knife, cut the chicken into bite-sized pieces. Add the chicken to the wok and cook, stirring frequently, until evenly browned.

3 Using a sharp knife, trim the okra.

4 Add the onion, garlic, and okra to the wok and cook for a further 2–3 minutes, stirring constantly.

5 Mix the curry paste with the chicken bouillon and lemon juice and pour over the mixture in the wok. Bring to a boil, cover, and leave to simmer for 30 minutes.

6 Coarsely grate the creamed coconut, stir it into the curry, and cook for about 5 minutes. The creamed coconut will help to thicken the juices.

7 Add the pineapple, yogurt, and cilantro and heat through for 2 minutes, stirring.

8 Garnish and serve hot with boiled rice.

3

5

cook's tip

Score around the top of the okra with a knife before cooking to release the sticky glue-like substance which is bitter in taste.

stir-fried chicken with chili & crispy basil

Chicken drumsticks are cooked in a delicious sauce and served with deep-fried basil for color and flavor.

Serves 4

8 chicken drumsticks

2 tbsp soy sauce

1 tbsp sunflower oil

1 red chile

3½ oz carrots, cut into thin stalks

6 celery stalks, cut into sticks

3 tbsp sweet chili sauce

oil, for frying

about 50 fresh basil leaves

1 Remove the skin from the chicken drumsticks if desired. Make 3 slashes in each drumstick. Brush the drumsticks with the soy sauce.

2 Heat the oil in a preheated wok and cook the drumsticks for 20 minutes, turning frequently, until they are cooked through.

3 Seed and finely chop the chile. Add the chile, carrots, and celery to the wok and cook for a further 5 minutes. Stir in the chili sauce, cover, and allow to bubble gently whilst preparing the basil leaves.

4 Heat a little oil in a heavy based pan. Carefully add the basil leaves—stand well away from the pan and protect your hand with a dish cloth as they may spit a little. Cook for about 30 seconds or until they begin to curl up but not brown. Transfer to paper towels to drain.

5 Arrange the cooked chicken, vegetables and pan juices on to a warm serving plate and garnish with the deep-fried crispy basil leaves.

1

3

1

cook's tip

Basil has a very strong flavor which is perfect with chicken and Chinese flavorings. You could use baby spinach instead of the basil, if you prefer.

savory chicken sausages

Served with a smooth creamy tomato sauce, this makes an excellent light lunch with freshly baked cheese bread.

Serves 4-6

3 cups fresh bread crumbs

9 oz cooked chicken, ground

1 small leek, chopped finely

pinch each of mixed herbs and mustard
   powder

salt and pepper

2 eggs, separated

4 tbsp milk

crisp bread crumbs for coating

2 tbsp beef drippings

1 In a large clean bowl, combine the fresh bread crumbs, ground chicken, leek, mixed herbs, and mustard powder, and season with salt and pepper. Mix together until thoroughly incorporated.

2 Add 1 whole egg and an egg yolk with a little milk to bind the mixture.

3 Divide the mixture into 6 or 8 and shape into thick or thin sausages.

4 Whisk the remaining egg white until frothy. Coat the sausages first in the egg white and then in the crisp bread crumbs.

5 Heat the drippings and sauté the sausages for 6 minutes until golden brown. Serve.

cook's tip

Make your own ground chicken by working lean cuts of chicken in a food processor.

variation

If you want to lower the saturated fat content of this recipe, use a little oil for frying instead of the drippings.

2

3

1

garlicky chicken cushions

Stuffed with creamy ricotta, spinach, and garlic, then gently cooked in a rich tomato sauce, this is a suitable dish to make ahead of time.

Serves 4

4 part-boned chicken breasts

½ cup frozen spinach, defrosted

½ cup ricotta cheese

2 garlic cloves, finely chopped

salt and pepper

1 tbsp olive oil

1 onion, chopped

1 red bell pepper, sliced

14 oz can chopped tomatoes

6 tbsp wine or chicken bouillon

10 stuffed olives, sliced

pasta, to serve

1 Make a slit between the skin and meat on one side of each chicken breast. Lift the skin to form a pocket, being careful to leave the skin attached to the other side.

2 Put the spinach into a strainer and press out the water with a spoon. Mix with the ricotta, half the garlic, and seasoning.

3 Spoon the spinach mixture under the skin of each chicken breast, then secure the edge of the skin with toothpicks.

4 Heat the oil in a skillet, add the onion, and sauté for a minute, stirring. Add the remaining garlic and red bell pepper and cook for 2 minutes. Stir in the tomatoes, wine, or bouillon, olives, and seasoning. Set the sauce aside and chill the chicken if preparing in advance.

5 Bring the sauce to a boil, pour into a shallow ovenproof dish and arrange the chicken breasts on top in a single layer.

3

5

6 Cook, uncovered in a preheated oven, 400°F, for 35 minutes until the chicken is golden and cooked through. Test by making a slit in one of the chicken breasts with a skewer to make sure the juices run clear and not pink. Spoon a little of the sauce over the chicken breasts then transfer to serving plates. Serve with pasta.

1

tom's toad in the hole

This unusual recipe uses chicken and Cumberland sausage, which is then made into individual bite-size cakes.

Serves 4-6

1 cup all-purpose flour

pinch of salt

1 egg, beaten

1 scant cup milk

⅓ cup water

2 tbsp beef drippings

9 oz chicken breasts

9 oz Cumberland sausage

chicken or onion gravy, to serve (optional)

1 Mix the flour and salt in a bowl, make a well in the center and add the beaten egg.

2 Add half the milk, and using a wooden spoon, work in the flour slowly.

3 Beat the mixture until smooth, then add the remaining milk and water.

4 Beat again until the mixture is smooth. Let the mixture stand for at least 1 hour.

5 Add the drippings to individual baking pans or to one large baking pan. Cut up the chicken and sausage so that you get a generous piece in each individual pan or several scattered around the large pan.

6 Heat in a preheated oven, 425°F, for 5 minutes until very hot. Remove the pans from the oven and pour in the batter, leaving space for the mixture to expand.

7 Return to the oven to cook for 35 minutes, until risen and golden brown. Do not open the oven door for at least 30 minutes.

8 Serve while hot, with chicken or onion gravy, or alone.

variation

Use skinless, boneless chicken legs instead of chicken breast in the recipe. Cut up as directed. Use your favorite variety of sausage instead of Cumberland sausage.

chicken strips & dips

Very simple to make and easy to eat with fingers, this dish can be served warm for a light lunch or cold as part of a buffet.

Serves 2

2 boneless chicken breasts

2 tbsp all-purpose flour

1 tbsp sunflower oil

PEANUT DIP

3 tbsp smooth or crunchy peanut butter

4 tbsp unsweetened yogurt

1 tsp grated orange peel

orange juice (optional)

TOMATO DIP

5 tbsp creamy fromage blanc

1 medium tomato

2 tsp tomato paste

1 tsp chopped fresh chives

1 Using a sharp knife, slice the chicken into fairly thin strips and toss in the flour to coat.

2 Heat the oil in a non-stick pan and sauté the chicken until golden and thoroughly cooked. Remove the chicken strips from the pan and drain well on paper towels.

3 To make the peanut dip, mix together all the ingredients in a bowl (if liked, add a little orange juice to thin the consistency).

4 To make the tomato dip, chop the tomato and mix with the remaining ingredients.

5 Serve the chicken strips with the dips and a selection of vegetable sticks for dipping.

variation

For a lower-fat alternative, poach the strips of chicken in a small amount of boiling chicken bouillon for 6–8 minutes.

variation

For a refreshing guacamole dip, combine 1 mashed avocado, 2 finely chopped scallions, 1 chopped tomato,1 crushed garlic clove, and a squeeze of lemon juice. Remember to add the lemon juice immediately after the avocado has been mashed to prevent discoloration.

1

2

4

chicken risotto alla milanese

This famous dish is known throughout the world, and it is perhaps the best known of all Italian risottos, although there are many variations.

Serves 4

½ cup butter

2 lb chicken meat, sliced thinly

1 large onion, chopped

2½ cups risotto rice

2½ cups chicken bouillon

⅔ cup white wine

1 tsp crumbled saffron

salt and pepper

½ cup grated Parmesan cheese, to serve

1

2

3

1 Heat 4 tbsp of butter in a deep skillet, and sauté the chicken, and onion until golden brown.

2 Add the rice, stir well, and cook for 15 minutes.

3 Heat the bouillon until boiling and gradually add to the rice. Add the white wine, saffron, salt, and pepper to taste and mix well. Simmer gently for 20 minutes, stirring occasionally, and adding more bouillon if the risotto becomes too dry.

4 Leave to stand for a few minutes and just before serving add a little more bouillon and simmer for a further 10 minutes. Serve the risotto, sprinkled with the grated Parmesan cheese and the remaining butter.

cook's tip

A risotto should have moist but separate grains. Bouillon should be added a little at a time and only when the last addition has been completely absorbed.

variation

The possibilities for risotto are endless—try adding the following just at the end of cooking time: cashew nuts and corn, lightly sautéed zucchini and basil, or artichokes and oyster mushrooms.

quick chicken bake

This recipe is a type of cottage pie and is just as versatile. Add vegetables and herbs of your choice, depending on what you have at hand.

Serves 4

1 lb 2 oz ground chicken

1 large onion, chopped finely

2 carrots, diced finely

2 tbsp all–purpose flour

1 tbsp tomato paste

1¼ cups chicken bouillon

salt and pepper

pinch of fresh thyme

2 lb potatoes, creamed with butter and milk and highly seasoned

¾ cup grated crumbly cheese

peas, to serve

3

4

1 Dry-fry the ground chicken, onion and carrots in a non-stick saucepan for 5 minutes, stirring frequently.

2 Sprinkle the chicken with the flour and simmer for a further 2 minutes.

3 Gradually blend in the tomato paste and bouillon then simmer for 15 minutes. Season and add the thyme.

5

4 Transfer the chicken and vegetable mixture to an ovenproof casserole and allow to cool.

5 Spoon the mashed potato over the chicken mixture and sprinkle with the cheese. Bake in a preheated oven, 400°F, for 20 minutes, or until the cheese is bubbling and golden, then serve with the peas.

variation

Try using a mixture of cheeses on top of this dish. Either use whatever variety of cheese you have to hand in the pantry or choose cheeses that melt easily to provide an extra tasty layer of melted cheese on top of the bake.

mediterranean chicken parcels

This method of cooking makes the chicken aromatic and succulent. It also reduces the amount of oil needed since the chicken and vegetables cook in their own juices.

Serves 6

1 tbsp olive oil

6 skinless chicken breast fillets

2 cups mozzarella cheese

3½ cups zucchini, sliced

6 large tomatoes, sliced

pepper

1 small bunch fresh basil or oregano

rice or pasta, to serve

 Cut six pieces of foil each about 10 inches square. Brush the foil squares lightly with oil and set aside until required.

2 With a sharp knife, slash each chicken breast at intervals, slice the mozzarella cheese, and place between the cuts in the chicken.

3 Divide the zucchini and tomatoes between the pieces of foil and sprinkle with pepper. Tear or roughly chop the basil or oregano and scatter over the vegetables in each packet.

4 Place the chicken on top of each pile of vegetables then wrap in the foil to enclose the chicken and vegetables, tucking in the ends.

5 Place on a cookie sheet and bake in a preheated oven, 400°F, for about 30 minutes.

6 To serve, unwrap each foil packet and serve with rice or pasta.

cook's tip

To aid cooking, place the vegetables and chicken on the shiny side of the foil so that once the packet is wrapped up the dull surface of the foil is facing outward. This ensures that the heat is absorbed into the packet and not reflected away from it.

golden chicken risotto

If you prefer, ordinary long grain rice can be used instead of risotto rice, but it won't give you the traditional, deliciously creamy texture that is typical of Italian risottos.

Serves 4

2 tbsp sunflower oil

1 tbsp butter or margarine

1 medium leek, thinly sliced

1 large yellow bell pepper, diced

3 skinless, boneless chicken breasts, diced

12 oz risotto rice

few strands saffron

salt and pepper

6¼ cups chicken bouillon

7 oz can corn

½ cup toasted unsalted peanuts

½ cup grated Parmesan cheese

1

2

1 Heat the oil and butter or margarine in a large pan. Sauté the leek and bell pepper for 1 minute then stir in the chicken and cook, stirring until golden brown.

2 Stir in the rice and cook for 2–3 minutes.

3 Stir in the saffron strands, and salt and pepper to taste. Add the bouillon, a little at a time, cover, and cook over a low heat, stirring occasionally, for about 20 minutes, until the rice is tender and most of the liquid is absorbed. Do not let the risotto dry out—add more bouillon if necessary.

4

4 Stir in the corn, peanuts, and Parmesan cheese, then adjust the seasoning to taste. Serve hot.

cook's tip

Risottos can be frozen, before adding the Parmesan cheese, for up to 1 month, but remember to reheat this risotto thoroughly as it contains chicken.

elizabethan chicken

Chicken is surprisingly delicious when combined with fruits such as grapes or gooseberries, which make a change to the more usual citrus fruits.

Serves 4

1 tbsp butter

1 tbsp sunflower oil

4 skinless, boneless chicken breasts

4 shallots, finely chopped

⅔ cup chicken bouillon

1 tbsp cider vinegar

1 cup halved pitless grapes

1/2 cup heavy cream

1 tsp freshly grated nutmeg

salt and pepper

cornstarch, to thicken (optional)

variation

If desired, add a little dry white wine or vermouth to the sauce in step 3.

1 Heat the butter and sunflower oil in a wide, flameproof casserole or pan and quickly sauté the chicken breasts until golden brown, turning once. Remove the chicken breasts and keep warm while you are cooking the shallots.

2 Add the chopped shallots to the pan and sauté gently until softened and lightly browned. Return the chicken breasts to the pan.

3 Add the chicken bouillon and cider vinegar to the pan, bring to a boil, cover, and simmer gently for 10–12 minutes, stirring occasionally.

3

1

4

4 Transfer the chicken to a serving dish. Add the grapes, cream, and nutmeg to the pan. Heat through, seasoning with salt and pepper to taste. Add a little cornstarch to thicken the sauce, if desired. Pour the sauce over the chicken and serve.

chicken lady jayne

If you prefer, just use boneless chicken breasts in this recipe. This dish has a surprising combination of coffee and brandy flavors.

1

Serves 4

4 chicken breasts or suprêmes,
   each about 4½ oz

4 tbsp corn oil

8 shallots, sliced

peel and juice of 1 lemon

2 tsp Worcestershire sauce

4 tbsp chicken bouillon

1 tbsp chopped fresh parsley

3 tbsp coffee liqueur

3 tbsp brandy, warmed

2

3

1 Place the chicken breasts or suprêmes on a chopping board, cover with plastic wrap and pound them until flattened with a meat mallet or rolling pin.

2 Heat the oil in a large skillet and sauté the chicken for 3 minutes on each side. Add the shallots and cook for a further 3 minutes.

3 Sprinkle with lemon juice and lemon peel and add the Worcestershire sauce and chicken bouillon. Cook for 2 minutes, then sprinkle with the chopped fresh parsley.

4 Add the coffee liqueur and the brandy and flame the chicken by lighting the spirit with a taper or long match. Cook until the flame is extinguished and serve.

cook's tip

A suprême is a chicken fillet that sometimes has part of the wing bone remaining. Chicken breasts can be used instead.

golden-glazed chicken

A glossy glaze with sweet and fruity flavors coats chicken breasts in this tasty recipe. The fresh minty rice complements the glaze perfectly.

Serves 6

6 boneless chicken breasts

1 tsp turmeric

1 tbsp whole–grain mustard

1¼ cups orange juice

2 tbsp honey

2 tbsp sunflower oil

1½ cups long grain rice

1 orange

3 tbsp chopped mint

salt and pepper

mint sprigs, to garnish

1 With a sharp knife, mark the surface of the chicken breasts in a diamond pattern. Mix together the turmeric, mustard, orange juice, and honey and pour over the chicken. Chill until required.

2 Lift the chicken from the marinade and pat dry on paper towels.

3 Heat the oil in a wide pan, add the chicken, and sauté until golden, turning once. Drain off any excess oil. Pour over the marinade, cover, and simmer for 10–15 minutes until the chicken is tender.

1

2

5

4 Boil the rice in lightly salted water until tender and drain well. Finely grate the peel from the orange and stir into the rice with the mint. Adjust seasoning to taste.

5 Using a sharp knife, remove the peel and white pith from the orange and cut the flesh into segments.

6 Serve the chicken with the orange and mint rice, garnished with orange segments and mint sprigs.

variation

To make a slightly sharper sauce, use a small grapefruit instead of the oranges.

harlequin chicken

This colorful, simple dish will tempt the appetites of all the family—it is ideal for toddlers, who enjoy the fun shapes of the multi-colored bell peppers.

Serves 4

10 skinless, boneless chicken thighs

1 medium onion

1 each medium red, green,
    and yellow bell peppers

1 tbsp sunflower oil

14 oz can chopped tomatoes

2 tbsp chopped fresh parsley

pepper

whole wheat bread and a green salad,
    to serve

---

cook's tip

If you are making this dish for small children, the chicken can be finely chopped or ground first.

cooks tip

You can use dried parsley instead of fresh but remember that you only need about one half of dried to fresh.

1 Using a sharp knife, cut the chicken thighs into bite-sized pieces.

2 Peel and thinly slice the onion. Halve and seed the bell peppers and cut into small diamond shapes.

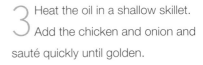

4

1

2

3 Heat the oil in a shallow skillet. Add the chicken and onion and sauté quickly until golden.

4 Add the bell peppers, cook for 2–3 minutes, stir in the tomatoes and parsley, and season with pepper.

5 Cover tightly and simmer for about 15 minutes, until the chicken and vegetables are tender. Serve hot with whole wheat bread and a green salad.

italian chicken spirals

Steaming allows you to cook without fat, and these little foil packets retain all the natural juices of the chicken while cooking conveniently over the pasta while it boils.

Serves 4

4 skinless, boneless, chicken breasts

1 cup fresh basil leaves

2 tbsp filberts

1 garlic clove, finely chopped

salt and pepper

2 cups whole wheat pasta spirals

2 sun-dried tomatoes or fresh tomatoes

1 tbsp lemon juice

1 tbsp olive oil

1 tbsp capers

½ cup black olives

variation

Sun-dried tomatoes have a wonderful, rich flavor, but if you can't find them, use fresh tomatoes.

1 Beat the chicken breasts with a rolling pin to flatten evenly.

2 Place the basil and filberts in a food processor and process until finely chopped. Mix with the garlic, salt, and pepper.

3 Spread the basil mixture over the chicken breasts and roll up from one short end to enclose the filling. Wrap the chicken rolls tightly in foil so that they hold their shape, then seal the ends well.

4 Bring a large pan of lightly salted water to a boil and cook the pasta until tender, but still firm to the bite.

5 Place the chicken packets in a steamer basket or colander set over the pan, cover tightly, and steam for 10 minutes. Meanwhile, dice the tomatoes.

6 Drain the pasta and return to the pan with the lemon juice, olive oil, tomatoes, capers, and olives. Heat through.

7 Pierce the chicken with a skewer to make sure that the juices run clear and not pink, then slice the chicken, arrange over the pasta, and serve.

deviled chicken

Chicken is spiked with cayenne pepper and paprika and finished off with a fruity sauce, which is a delicate pink colour.

Serves 2-3

¼ cup all-purpose flour

1 tbsp cayenne pepper

1 tsp paprika

12 oz skinless, boneless chicken, diced

2 tbsp butter

1 onion, chopped finely

1⅛ cups milk, warmed

4 tbsp apple paste

¾ cup white grapes

⅔ cup soured cream

sprinkle of paprika

1 Mix the flour, cayenne pepper, and paprika together and use to coat the chicken.

2 Shake off any excess flour. Melt the butter in a pan and gently sauté the chicken with the onion for 4 minutes.

3 Stir in the flour and spice mixture. Add the milk slowly, stirring until the sauce thickens.

4 Simmer until the sauce is smooth.

5 Add the apple paste and grapes and simmer gently for 20 minutes.

6 Transfer the chicken and devilled sauce to a serving dish and top with soured cream and a sprinkle of paprika.

variation

For a healthier alternative to soured cream, use unsweetened yogurt.

cooks tip

Add more paprika if desired. As it is quite a mild spice, you can add plenty without it being too overpowering.

1

3

5

steamed chicken & spring vegetable packets

A healthy recipe with a delicate Asian flavor, ideal for tender young summer vegetables. Use large, fresh spinach leaves to wrap around the chicken.

1

Serves 4

4 boneless, skinless chicken breasts

1 tsp ground lemongrass

salt and pepper

2 scallions, chopped finely

1 cup young carrots

1¾ cups young zucchini

2 stalks celery

1 tsp light soy sauce

¾ cup spinach leaves

2 tsp sesame oil

1 With a sharp knife, make a slit through one side of each chicken breast, to open out a large pocket. Sprinkle the inside of the pocket with lemongrass, salt, and pepper. Tuck the scallions into the pockets.

2 Trim the carrots, zucchini, and celery and cut into small matchsticks. Plunge them into a pan of boiling water for 1 minute, drain, and toss in the soy sauce.

2

3

3 Pack the vegetables into the pockets in each chicken breast and fold over firmly to enclose. Reserve any remaining vegetables. Wash the spinach leaves thoroughly, drain, and pat dry with paper towels. Wrap the chicken breasts firmly in the spinach leaves to enclose completely. If the leaves are too firm to wrap the chicken easily, steam them for a few seconds until they are softened and flexible.

4 Place the wrapped chicken in a steamer and steam over rapidly boiling water for 20–25 minutes, depending on size.

5 Stir-fry any leftover vegetable sticks and spinach for 1–2 minutes in the sesame oil and serve with the chicken.

prosciutto-wrapped chicken packets

Stuffed with creamy ricotta, nutmeg, and spinach, then wrapped with wafer thin slices of prosciutto and gently cooked in white wine.

Serves 4

½ cup frozen spinach, defrosted

½ cup ricotta cheese

pinch grated nutmeg

salt and pepper

4 skinless, boneless chicken breasts,
   each weighing 6 oz

4 prosciutto slices

2 tbsp butter

1 tbsp olive oil

12 small onions or shallots

1½ cups white mushrooms, sliced

1 tbsp all-purpose flour

⅔ cup dry white or red wine

1¼ cups chicken bouillon

carrot paste and green beans,
   to serve (optional)

1 Put the spinach into a strainer and press out the water with a spoon. Mix with the ricotta and nutmeg and season with salt and pepper to taste.

2 Using a sharp knife, slit each chicken breast through the side and enlarge each cut to form a pocket. Fill with the spinach mixture, reshape the chicken breasts, wrap each breast tightly in a slice of ham, and secure with toothpicks. Cover and chill in the refrigerator.

3 Heat the butter and oil in a skillet and brown the chicken breasts for 2 minutes on each side. Transfer the chicken to a large, shallow ovenproof dish and keep warm until required.

4 Sauté the onions and mushrooms for 2–3 minutes until lightly browned. Stir in the all-purpose flour then gradually add the wine and bouillon. Bring to a boil, stirring constantly. Season and spoon the mixture around the chicken.

5 Cook the chicken uncovered in a preheated oven, 400°F, for 20 minutes. Turn the breasts over and cook for a further 10 minutes. Remove the toothpicks and serve with the sauce, together with carrot paste and green beans, if wished.

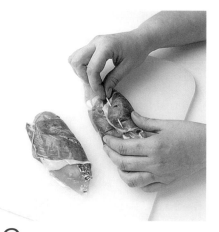

2

3

4

chicken with two bell pepper sauce

This quick and simple dish is colorful and healthy. It would be perfect for an impromptu lunch or supper dish.

1

3

4

Serves 4

2 tbsp olive oil

2 medium onions, chopped finely

2 garlic cloves, finely chopped

2 red bell peppers, chopped

good pinch cayenne pepper

2 tsp tomato paste

2 yellow bell peppers, chopped

pinch of dried basil

salt and pepper

4 skinless, boneless chicken breasts

⅔ cup dry white wine

⅔ cup chicken bouillon

bouquet garni

fresh herbs, to garnish

cook's tip

Make your own bouquet garni by tying together sprigs of your favorite herbs with string, or wrap up dried herbs in a piece of muslin. A popular combination is thyme, parsley, and bay.

1 Heat 1 tablespoon of oil in each of two medium-sized pans. Place half the chopped onions, 1 of the garlic cloves, the red bell peppers, the cayenne pepper, and the tomato paste in one of the pans. Place the remaining onion, garlic, yellow bell peppers, and basil in the other pan.

2 Cover each pan and cook over a very low heat for 1 hour until the bell peppers are soft. If either mixture becomes dry, add a little water. Work each mixture separately in a food processor, then sift separately.

3 Return the separate mixtures to the pans and season. The two sauces can be gently reheated while the chicken is cooking.

4 Put the chicken breasts into a skillet and add the wine and bouillon. Add the bouquet garni and bring the liquid to simmer. Cook the chicken for about 20 minutes until tender.

5 To serve, pour a serving of each sauce on to four serving plates, slice the chicken breasts, and arrange on the plates. Garnish with fresh herbs.

poached breast of chicken with whiskey

After cooking with bouillon and vegetables, chicken breasts are served with a velvety sauce made from whiskey and unsweetened yogurt.

Serves 6

2 tbsp butter

½ cup shredded leeks

⅓ cup diced carrot

¼ cup diced celery

4 shallots, sliced

2½ cups chicken bouillon

6 chicken breasts

¼ cup whiskey

1 scant cup unsweetened yogurt

2 tbsp freshly grated horseradish

1 tsp honey, warmed

1 tsp chopped fresh parsley

salt and pepper

sprig of fresh parsley, to garnish

1

5

3

1 Melt the butter in a large pan and add the leeks, carrot, celery, and shallots. Cook for 3 minutes, add half the chicken bouillon, and cook for about 8 minutes.

2 Add the remaining chicken bouillon, bring to a boil, add the chicken breasts, and cook for 10 minutes.

3 Remove the chicken and thinly slice. Place on a large, hot serving dish and keep warm until required.

4 In another pan, heat the whiskey until reduced by half. Strain the chicken bouillon through a fine sifter, add to the pan, and reduce the liquid by half.

5 Add the yogurt, the horseradish, and the honey. Heat gently and add the chopped parsley and salt and pepper to taste. Stir until well blended.

6 Pour a little of the whiskey sauce around the chicken and pour the remaining sauce into a sauceboat to serve.

7 Serve with a vegetable patty made from the leftover vegetables, mashed potato, and fresh vegetables. Garnish with the parsley sprig.

Long, slow cooking means meltingly succulent meat with a good, rich flavor. Because chicken itself does not have a strong flavour, it marries happily with almost any other ingredient, herb, or spice. The recipes in this section are drawn from many cuisines from around the world, and there are dishes from Italy, France, Hungary, the Caribbean, as well as the USA. French classics include Bourguignonne of Chicken and Brittany Chicken

Casserole. The aroma of roasting chicken is always tempting and this section includes the traditional roast chicken, with all the trimmings, as well as many other imaginative treatments. Unusual stuffings to try are zucchini and lime, marmalade, or oat and herb stuffing.

Many of the recipes in this section exploit the complementary flavours of chicken and fruits and there are some enticing taste combinations including cranberries, black cherries, apples, peaches, oranges, and mangoes.

roasts& casseroles

roast chicken in wild mushroom sauce

This unusual chicken dish has the flavor of roast chicken but is finished off in a casserole with a wild mushroom sauce.

Serves 4

⅓ cup butter, softened

1 garlic clove, crushed

salt and pepper

1 large chicken

2¼ cups wild mushrooms

12 shallots

2 tbsp all-purpose flour

⅔ cup brandy

1¼ cups heavy cream

1 tbsp chopped fresh parsley, to garnish

wild rice or roast potatoes, and green beans,
   to serve

2

1 Place the butter, garlic, and salt and
pepper in a bowl and combine well.

2 Rub the mixture inside and
outside of the chicken and leave
for 2 hours.

3 Place the chicken in a large roasting
pan and roast in the center of a
preheated oven, 450°F, for 1½ hours,
basting with garlic butter every ten
minutes.

4 Remove the chicken from the
roasting pan and set aside to
cool slightly.

5 Transfer the chicken juices to a
saucepan and cook the mushrooms
and shallots for 5 minutes. Sprinkle with
the flour. Add the warm brandy and
ignite using a taper or long match.

6 Add the heavy cream and cook for
3 minutes on a very low heat,
stirring all the time.

5

6

7 Remove the bones and cut the
chicken into small bite–size pieces,
then place the meat in a casserole dish.
Cover with the mushroom sauce and
bake in the oven, with the heat reduced
to 325°F for a further 12 minutes. Garnish
with the parsley and serve with wild rice
or roast potatoes and green beans.

suprême of chicken with black cherries

This recipe is rather time-consuming but it is well worth the effort. Cherries and chicken make a good flavor combination.

Serves 6

6 large chicken suprêmes

6 black peppercorns, crushed

2 cups pitted black cherries, or canned
  pitted cherries

12 shallots, sliced

4 slices rindless, streaky bacon, chopped

8 juniper berries

4 tbsp port

⅔ cup red wine

salt and pepper

2 tbsp butter

2 tbsp walnut oil

¼ cup flour

new potatoes and green beans, to serve

1

4

6 Cover with foil and bake in a preheated oven, 350°F, for 20 minutes. Transfer the chicken from the baking pan to a warm serving dish. Add the flour to the juices in the skillet and cook for 4 minutes, add the marinade, and bring to the boil then simmer for 10 minutes until the sauce reaches a smooth consistency.

7 Pour the cherry sauce over the chicken suprêmes and serve with new potatoes and green beans.

1 Place the chicken in an ovenproof dish. Add the peppercorns, cherries, or canned cherries and their juice, if using, and the shallots.

2 Add the bacon, juniper berries, port, and red wine. Season well.

3 Place the chicken in the refrigerator and leave to marinate for 48 hours.

4 Heat the butter and walnut oil in a large skillet. Remove the chicken from the marinade and sauté quickly in the pan for 4 minutes on each side.

5 Return the chicken to the marinade, reserving the butter, oil, and juices in the pan.

5

chicken marengo

Napoleon's chef was ordered to cook a sumptuous meal on the eve of the battle o
Marengo. He gathered everything possible to make a feast, and this was the result

1

Serves 4

8 chicken pieces

1 tbsp olive oil

10½ oz tomato paste

¾ cup white wine

2 tsp dried mixed herbs

1½ oz butter, melted

2 garlic cloves, crushed

8 slices white bread

3½ oz mixed mushrooms
    (such as white, oyster, and ceps)

1¾ oz black olives, chopped

1 tsp sugar

fresh basil, to garnish

3

4

1 Using a sharp knife, remove the bone from each of the chicken pieces.

2 Heat the oil in a large skillet. Add the chicken pieces and cook for 4–5 minutes, turning occasionally, or until browned all over.

3 Add the tomato paste, wine, and mixed herbs to the skillet. Bring to the boil and then leave to simmer for 30 minutes or until the chicken is tender and the juices run clear when a skewer is inserted into the thickest part of the meat.

4 To make the bruschetta, mix the melted butter and crushed garlic together. Lightly toast the slices of bread and brush with the garlic butter.

5 Add the remaining oil to a separate skillet and cook the mushrooms for 2–3 minutes or until just brown.

6 Add the olives and sugar to the chicken mixture and warm through.

7 Transfer the chicken and sauce to serving plates. Garnish with basil. Serve with the bruschetta and cooked mushrooms.

cook's tip

If you have time, marinate the chicken pieces in the wine and herbs and leave in the refrigerator for 2 hours. This will make the chicken more tender and accentuate the wine flavor of the sauce.

country chicken braise with rosemary dumplings

Root vegetables are always cheap and nutritious, and combined with chicken they make tasty and economical casseroles.

Serves 4

4 chicken quarters

2 tbsp sunflower oil

2 medium leeks

1 cup carrots, chopped

2 cups parsnips, chopped

2 small turnips, chopped

2½ cups chicken bouillon

3 tbsp Worcestershire sauce

2 sprigs fresh rosemary

salt and pepper

DUMPLINGS

1¾ cups self-rising flour

3½ oz shredded suet

1 tbsp chopped rosemary leaves

cold water, to mix

1 Remove the skin from the chicken if you prefer. Heat the oil in a large, flameproof casserole or heavy pan and sauté the chicken until golden. Using a draining spoon, remove the chicken from the pan. Drain off the excess fat.

2 Trim and slice the leeks. Add the carrots, parsnips, and turnips to the casserole and cook for 5 minutes, until lightly colored. Return the chicken to the pan.

3 Add the chicken bouillon, Worcestershire sauce, rosemary, and seasoning, then bring to the boil.

4 Reduce the heat, cover and simmer gently for about 50 minutes or until the juices run clear when the chicken is pierced with a skewer.

5 To make the dumplings, combine the flour, suet, and rosemary leaves with salt and pepper in a bowl. Stir in just enough cold water to bind to a firm dough.

6 Form into 8 small balls and place on top of the chicken and vegetables. Cover and simmer for a further 10–12 minutes, until the dumplings are well risen. Serve with the casserole.

brittany chicken casserole

A hearty, one-dish meal that would make a substantial lunch or supper. As it requires a long cooking time, make double quantities and freeze half to eat later.

Serves 6

2½ cups beans, such as flageolets,
    soaked overnight and drained

2 tbsp butter

2 tbsp olive oil

3 rindless bacon slices, chopped

1¾ lb chicken pieces

1 tbsp all-purpose flour

1¼ cups cider

⅔ cup chicken bouillon

salt and pepper

14 shallots

2 tbsp honey, warmed

8 oz ready-cooked beet

1 Cook the chosen beans in salted boiling water for about 25 minutes.

2 Heat the butter and olive oil in a flameproof casserole, add the bacon and chicken, and cook for 5 minutes.

3 Sprinkle with the flour then add the cider and chicken bouillon, stirring constantly to avoid lumps forming. Season with salt and pepper to taste and bring to the boil.

4 Add the beans then cover the casserole tightly with a lid or cooking foil and bake in the center of a preheated oven, 325°F, for 2 hours.

5 About 15 minutes before the end of cooking time, remove the lid or cooking foil from the casserole.

6 In a skillet, gently cook the shallots and honey together for 5 minutes, turning the shallots frequently.

7 Add the shallots and cooked beet to the casserole and leave to finish cooking in the oven for the last 15 minutes.

cook's tip

To save time, use canned flageolet beans instead of dried. Drain and rinse before adding to the chicken.

3

4

6

chicken with shallots in ginger sauce

This recipe has an Asian flavor, which can be further enhanced with chopped scallions, cinnamon, and lemongrass.

2

4

Serves 6-8

6 tbsp sesame oil

1¾ lb chicken meat

½ cup flour, seasoned

32 shallots, sliced

6 cups wild mushrooms, roughly chopped

1¼ cups chicken bouillon

2 tbsp Worcestershire sauce

1 tbsp honey

2 tbsp grated fresh gingerroot

salt and pepper

⅔ cup yogurt

flat leaf parsley, to garnish

wild rice and white rice, to serve

1 Heat the oil in a large skillet. Coat the chicken in the seasoned flour and cook for about 4 minutes, until browned all over. Transfer to a large deep casserole and keep warm until required.

2 Slowly cook the shallots and mushrooms in the juices.

3 Add the chicken bouillon, Worcestershire sauce, honey, and fresh gingerroot, then season.

4 Pour the mixture over the chicken, and cover the casserole with a lid or cooking foil.

5 Cook in the center of a preheated oven, 300°F, for about 1½ hours, until the meat is very tender. Add the yogurt and cook for a further 10 minutes. Serve the casserole with a mixture of wild rice and white rice and garnish with fresh parsley.

cook's tip

Mushrooms can be stored in the refrigerator for 24-36 hours. Keep them in paper bags as they "sweat" in plastic. You do not need to peel mushrooms but wild mushrooms must be washed thoroughly.

1

spiced chicken casserole

Spices, herbs, fruit, nuts, and vegetables are combined to make an appealing casserole with lots of flavor.

Serves 4-6

3 tbsp olive oil

2 lb chicken meat, sliced

10 shallots or pickling onions

3 carrots, chopped

½ cup chestnuts, sliced

½ cup slivered almonds, toasted

1 tsp freshly grated nutmeg

3 tsp ground cinnamon

1¼ cups white wine

1¼ cups chicken bouillon

¼ cup white wine vinegar

1 tbsp chopped fresh tarragon

1 tbsp chopped fresh flat leaf parsley

1 tbsp chopped fresh thyme

grated peel of 1 orange

1 tbsp dark muscovado sugar

sea salt and pepper

¾ cup pitless black grapes, halved

fresh herbs, to garnish

wild rice or puréed potato, to serve

1

2

3

1 Heat the olive oil in a large pan and sauté the chicken, shallots or pickling onions, and carrots for about 6 minutes or until browned.

2 Add the remaining ingredients, except the grapes, and simmer over a low heat for 2 hours until the meat is very tender. Stir the casserole occasionally.

3 Add the grapes just before serving. Garnish with herbs and serve with wild rice or puréed potato.

variation

Experiment with different types of nuts and fruits—try sunflower seeds instead of the almonds, and add 2 fresh apricots, chopped.

cook's tip

This casserole would also be delicious served with thick slices of crusty whole wheat bread to soak up the sauce.

chicken with baby onions & green peas

Pork fat adds a tasty flavor to this dish. If you can't find fresh garden peas, frozen peas are a good substitute.

Serves 4

1 cup pork fat, cut into small cubes

4 tbsp butter

16 small onions or shallots

2 lb 4 oz boneless chicken pieces

¼ cup all-purpose flour

2½ cups chicken bouillon

bouquet garni

4 cups fresh peas

salt and pepper

4

6

6 Remove the bouquet garni about 10 minutes before the end of cooking time and add the peas and the reserved pork and onions. Stir to mix and season to taste.

7 When cooked, place the chicken pieces on to a large platter, surrounded with the pork, peas, and onions.

1 Bring a saucepan of salted water to the boil and simmer the pork fat cubes for three minutes. Drain and dry the pork on paper towels.

2 Melt the butter in a large skillet, add the pork and onions, and sauté gently for 3 minutes until lightly browned.

2

3 Remove the pork and onions from the pan and set aside until required. Add the chicken pieces to the pan and cook until browned all over. Transfer the chicken to an ovenproof casserole.

4 Add the flour to the pan and cook, stirring until it begins to brown, then slowly blend in the chicken bouillon.

5 Cook the chicken, with the sauce and bouquet garni, in a preheated oven, 400°F, for 35 minutes.

cook's tip

If you want to cut down on fat, use lean bacon, cut into small cubes, rather than pork fat.

sage chicken & rice

Cooking in a single pot means that all of the flavors are retained. This is a substantial meal that needs only a salad and some crusty bread.

Serves 4

1 large onion, chopped

1 garlic clove, finely chopped

2 stalks celery, sliced

2 carrots, diced

2 sprigs fresh sage

1¼ cups chicken bouillon

12 oz boneless, skinless chicken breasts

1⅓ cups mixed brown and wild rice

14 oz can chopped tomatoes

dash of Tabasco sauce

salt and pepper

2 medium zucchini, trimmed and thinly sliced

3½ oz lean ham, diced

fresh sage, to garnish

crusty bread and salad leaves, to serve

cook's tip

If you do not have fresh sage, use 1 tsp of dried sage in step 1.

2

1 Place the onion, garlic, celery, carrots, and sprigs of fresh sage in a large pan and pour in the chicken bouillon. Bring to the boil, cover the pan, and simmer for 5 minutes.

2 Cut the chicken into 1 inch cubes and stir into the pan with the vegetables. Cover the pan and continue to cook for a further 5 minutes.

3 Stir in the rice and chopped tomatoes. Add a dash of Tabasco sauce to taste and season well. Bring to the boil, cover, and simmer for 25 minutes.

4 Stir in the sliced zucchini and diced ham and continue to cook, uncovered, for a further 10 minutes, stirring occasionally, until the rice is just tender.

5 Remove and discard the sprigs of sage. Garnish with a few sage leaves and serve with salad leaves and crusty bread.

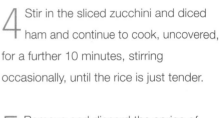

3

4

rustic chicken & orange pot

Low in fat and high in fiber, this colorful casserole makes a healthy and hearty meal. The bread topping soakes up the tasty cooking juices.

Serves 4

8 chicken drumsticks, skinned

1 tbsp whole wheat flour

1 tbsp olive oil

2 medium red onions

1 garlic clove, crushed

1 tsp fennel seeds

1 bay leaf

finely grated peel and juice of 1 small orange

14 oz can chopped tomatoes

14 oz can cannellini or flageolet beans, drained

salt and black pepper

3 thick slices whole wheat bread

2 tsp olive oil

2

3

5

1 Toss the chicken drumsticks in the flour to coat evenly. Heat the oil in a non–stick or heavy pan and sauté the chicken over a fairly high heat, turning frequently, until golden brown. Transfer to a large ovenproof casserole and keep warm until required.

2 Slice the red onions into thin wedges. Add to the pan and cook for a few minutes until lightly browned. Stir in the garlic.

3 Add the fennel seeds, bay leaf, orange peel and juice, tomatoes, beans, and seasoning.

4 Cover tightly and cook in a preheated oven, 375°F, for 30–35 minutes until the chicken juices are clear and not pink when pierced through the thickest part with a metal skewer.

5 For the topping, cut the bread into small dice and toss in the oil. Remove the lid from the casserole and top with the bread cubes. Bake for a further 15–20 minutes until the bread is golden and crisp. Serve hot.

cook's tip

Choose beans which are canned in water, with no added sugar or salt. Drain and rinse well before use.

chicken & plum casserole

Full of the flavors of fall, this combination of lean chicken, shallots, garlic, and fresh, juicy plums is a very fruity blend. Serve with bread to mop up the gravy.

Serves 4

2 rashers lean back bacon, rinds removed, trimmed and chopped

1 tbsp sunflower oil

1 lb skinless, boneless chicken thighs, cut into 4 equal strips

1 garlic clove, crushed

6 oz shallots, halved

8 oz plums, halved or quartered (if large) and stoned

1 tbsp light muscovado sugar

⅔ cup dry sherry

2 tbsp plum sauce

2 cups fresh chicken bouillon

2 tsp cornstarch mixed with 4 tsp cold water

2 tbsp fresh parsley, chopped, to garnish

crusty bread, to serve

variation

Chunks of lean turkey or pork would also go well with this combination of flavors. The cooking time will remain the same.

1

2

1 In a large, non-stick skillet, dry fry the bacon for 2–3 minutes until the juices run out. Remove the bacon from the pan with a draining spoon, set aside, and keep warm.

2 In the same skillet, heat the oil and sauté the chicken with the garlic and shallots for 4–5 minutes, stirring occasionally, until well browned all over.

3 Return the bacon to the pan and stir in the plums, sugar, sherry, plum sauce, and bouillon. Bring to the boil and simmer for 20 minutes until the plums have softened and the chicken is cooked through.

4 Add the cornstarch mixture to the pan and cook, stirring, for a further 2–3 minutes until thickened.

5 Spoon the casserole on to warm serving plates and garnish with chopped parsley. Serve with chunks of bread to mop up the fruity gravy.

3

rich mediterranean chicken casserole

A colorful casserole packed with sunshine flavors from the Mediterranean. Sun-dried tomatoes add a wonderful richness and you need very few to make this dish really special.

Serves 4

8 chicken thighs

2 tbsp olive oil

1 medium red onion, sliced

2 garlic cloves, crushed

1 large red bell pepper, sliced thickly

thinly pared rind and juice of 1 small orange

½ cup chicken bouillon

14 oz can chopped tomatoes

½ cup sun-dried tomatoes, thinly sliced

1 tbsp chopped fresh thyme

½ cup pitted black olives

salt and pepper

thyme sprigs and orange peel, to garnish

crusty fresh bread, to serve

cook's tip

Sun-dried tomatoes have a dense texture and concentrated taste, and add intense flavor to slow-cooking casseroles.

1

2

1 In a heavy or non-stick large skillet, sauté the chicken without fat over a fairly high heat, turning occasionally until golden brown. Using a draining spoon, drain off any excess fat from the chicken and transfer to a flameproof casserole.

2 Sauté the onion, garlic, and bell pepper in the pan over a moderate heat for 3–4 minutes. Transfer to the casserole.

3 Add the orange peel and juice, chicken bouillon, canned tomatoes, and sun-dried tomatoes and stir to combine.

4 Bring to the boil then cover the casserole with a lid and simmer very gently over a low heat for about 1 hour, stirring occasionally. Add the chopped fresh thyme and pitted black olives, then adjust the seasoning with salt and pepper.

5 Scatter orange peel and thyme over the casserole to garnish, and serve with crusty bread.

3

garlic chicken casserole

This is a cassoulet with a twist—it is made with chicken instead of duck and lamb. Save time by using canned beans, such as borlotti or cannellini beans which are both good in this dish.

Serves 4

4 tbsp sunflower oil

1¾ lb chicken meat, chopped

3 cups mushrooms, sliced

16 shallots

6 garlic cloves, finely chopped

1 tbsp all-purpose flour

1 cup white wine

1 cup chicken bouillon

1 bouquet garni (1 bay leaf, sprig thyme,
   celery, parsley, and sage tied together
   with string)

salt and pepper

14 oz can borlotti beans

small squash, to serve

3

5

2

4 Add the white wine and chicken bouillon, stir until boiling, then add the bouquet garni. Season well with salt and pepper.

5 Drain the borlotti beans and rinse thoroughly, then add to the casserole.

6 Cover and place in the center of a preheated oven, 300°F, for 2 hours. Remove the bouquet garni and serve the casserole with small squash.

1 Heat the sunflower oil in an ovenproof casserole and sauté the chicken until browned all over. Remove the chicken from the casserole with a draining spoon and set aside until required.

2 Add the mushrooms, shallots, and garlic to the fat in the casserole and cook for 4 minutes.

3 Return the chicken to the casserole and sprinkle with the flour, then cook for a further 2 minutes.

cook's tip

Mushrooms are ideal in a low-fat diet because they are high in flavor and contain no fat. Experiment with the wealth of varieties that are now available from stores.

cook's tip

Serve the casserole with whole wheat rice to make this filling dish go even further.

179

bourguignonne of chicken

A recipe based on a classic French dish. Use a good quality wine when making this casserole and you can serve it to the most discerning diners.

Serves 4-6

4 tbsp sunflower oil

1¾ lb chicken meat, diced

3 cups white mushrooms

⅔ cup rindless, smoked bacon, diced

16 shallots

2 garlic cloves, crushed

1 tbsp all-purpose flour

⅔ cup white Burgundy wine

⅔ cup chicken bouillon

1 bouquet garni (1 bay leaf, sprig thyme, stick of celery, parsley, and sage tied with string)

salt and pepper

deep-fried croutons and a selection of cooked vegetables, to serve

cook's tip

A good quality red wine can be used instead of the white wine, to produce a rich, glossy red sauce.

1

2

3

1 Heat the sunflower oil in an ovenproof casserole and brown the chicken all over. Remove from the casserole with a slotted spoon.

2 Add the mushrooms, bacon, shallots, and garlic to the casserole and cook for 4 minutes.

3 Return the chicken to the casserole and sprinkle with flour. Cook for a further 2 minutes, stirring.

4 Add the Burgundy wine and chicken bouillon to the casserole and stir until boiling. Add the bouquet garni and season well with salt and pepper.

5 Cover the casserole and bake in the center of a preheated oven, 200°F, for 1½ hours. Remove the bouquet garni.

6 Deep fry 8 heart–shaped croutons in beef drippings and serve with the bourguignonne.

hungarian chicken goulash

Goulash is traditionally made with beef, but this recipe successfully uses chicken instead. To reduce fat, use a low-fat cream in place of the soured cream.

Serves 6

1¾ lb chicken meat, diced

½ cup flour, seasoned with 1 tsp paprika,
  salt and pepper

2 tbsp olive oil

2 tbsp butter

1 onion, sliced

24 shallots, peeled

1 each red and green bell pepper, chopped

1 tbsp paprika

1 tsp rosemary, crushed

4 tbsp tomato paste

1¼ cups chicken bouillon

⅔ cup claret

14 oz can chopped tomatoes

⅔ cup soured cream

1 tbsp chopped fresh parsley, to garnish

chunks of bread and a side salad, to serve

2

3

4

1 Toss the chicken in the seasoned flour until it is coated all over.

2 In a flameproof casserole, heat the oil and butter and sauté the onion, shallots, and bell peppers for 3 minutes.

3 Add the chicken and cook for a further 4 minutes.

4 Sprinkle with the paprika and rosemary.

5 Add the tomato paste, chicken bouillon, claret, and chopped tomatoes, cover, and cook in the center of a preheated oven, 325°F for 1½ hours.

6 Remove the casserole from the oven, allow it to stand for 4 minutes, add the soured cream, and garnish with parsley.

7 Serve with chunks of bread and a side salad.

variation

Serve the goulash with buttered ribbon noodles instead of bread. For an authentic touch, try a Hungarian red wine instead of the claret.

old english chicken stewed in ale

This is a slow-cooked, old-fashioned stew to warm up a wintry day. The rarebit toasts are a perfect accompaniment to soak up the rich juices, but if you prefer, serve the stew with jacket potatoes.

Serves 4-6

4 large, skinless chicken thighs

2 tbsp all-purpose flour

2 tbsp English mustard powder

2 tbsp sunflower oil

1 tbsp butter

4 small onions

2½ cups beer

2 tbsp Worcestershire sauce

salt and pepper

3 tbsp chopped fresh sage leaves

RAREBIT TOASTS

½ cup grated hard English Cheddar

1 tsp English mustard powder

1 tsp all-purpose flour

1 tsp Worcestershire sauce

1 tbsp beer

2 slices whole wheat toast

green vegetables and new potatoes,
    to serve

1

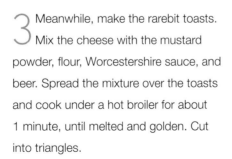

2

3

1 Trim any excess fat from the chicken and toss in the flour and mustard powder to coat evenly. Heat the sunflower oil and butter in a large flameproof casserole and sauté the chicken over a fairly high heat, turning occasionally, until golden. Remove the chicken from the casserole with a draining spoon and keep hot.

2 Peel the onions and slice into wedges, then sauté quickly until golden. Add the chicken, beer, Worcestershire sauce, and salt and pepper to taste. Bring to the boil, cover, and simmer very gently for about 1½ hours, until the chicken is very tender.

3 Meanwhile, make the rarebit toasts. Mix the cheese with the mustard powder, flour, Worcestershire sauce, and beer. Spread the mixture over the toasts and cook under a hot broiler for about 1 minute, until melted and golden. Cut into triangles.

4 Stir the sage leaves into the chicken stew, bring to the boil, and serve with the rarebit toasts, a green vegetable and new potatoes.

cook's tip

If you do not have fresh sage, use 2 tsp of dried sage in step 2.

fricassée of chicken in lime sauce

The addition of lime juice and lime peel adds a delicious tangy flavor to this chicken stew. The bell peppers add colour and flavor.

Serves 4

1 large chicken, cut into small portions

½ cup flour, seasoned

2 tbsp oil

1 lb 2 oz baby onions or shallots, sliced

1 each green and red bell pepper,
    thinly sliced

⅔ cup chicken bouillon

juice and peel of 2 limes

2 chiles, chopped

2 tbsp oyster sauce

1 tsp Worcestershire sauce

salt and pepper

1 Coat the chicken pieces in the seasoned flour. Heat the oil in a large skillet and cook the chicken for about 4 minutes until browned all over.

2 Using a draining spoon, transfer the chicken to a large, deep casserole and sprinkle with the sliced onions. Keep warm until required.

3 Slowly sauté the bell peppers in the juices remaining in the skillet.

4 Add the chicken bouillon, lime juice, and peel, and cook for a further 5 minutes.

5 Add the chiles, oyster sauce, and Worcestershire sauce. Season with salt and pepper to taste.

6 Pour the bell peppers and juices over the chicken and onions.

7 Cover the casserole with a lid or cooking foil.

8 Cook in the center of a preheated oven, 375°F, for 1½ hours until the chicken is very tender, then serve.

cook's tip

Try this casserole with a cheese biscuit topping. About 30 minutes before the end of cooking time, simply top with rounds cut from cheese biscuit pastry.

2

4

6

jamaican hotch-potch

A tasty way to make chicken joints go a long way, this hearty casserole, spiced with the warm, subtle flavor of ginger, is a good choice for a Halloween party.

Serves 4

2 tsp sunflower oil

4 chicken drumsticks

4 chicken thighs

1 medium onion

1 lb 10 oz piece squash or pumpkin, diced

1 green bell pepper, sliced

1 inch fresh ginger root, finely chopped

14 oz can chopped tomatoes

1¼ cups chicken bouillon

¼ cup split lentils

garlic salt and cayenne pepper

2 oz can corn

crusty bread, to serve

2

2

2

2

1 Heat the oil in a large flameproof casserole and sauté the chicken joints until golden, turning frequently.

2 Using a sharp knife, peel and slice the onion, peel and dice the squash or pumpkin, and seed and slice the bell pepper.

3 Drain any excess fat from the pan and add the prepared onion, pumpkin, and pepper. Gently sauté for a few minutes until lightly browned. Add the chopped ginger root, tomatoes, chicken bouillon, and lentils. Season lightly with garlic salt and cayenne pepper.

4 Cover the casserole and place in a preheated oven, 375°F, for about 1 hour, until the vegetables are tender and the chicken juices run clear if pierced with a skewer.

5 Add the drained corn and cook for a further 5 minutes. Season to taste and serve with crusty bread.

variation

If you can't find fresh ginger root, add 1 tsp allspice for a warm, fragrant aroma.

cook's tip

If squash or pumpkin is not available, rutabaga makes a good substitute.

country chicken hotch-potch

There are many regional versions of hotch-potch, all using fresh, local ingredients. Now, there is an endless variety of ingredients available all year, perfect for traditional one-pot cooking.

Serves 4

4 chicken quarters

6 medium potatoes, cut into ¼ inch slices

salt and pepper

2 sprigs thyme

2 sprigs rosemary

2 bay leaves

1 cup rindless, smoked streaky bacon,
    diced

1 large onion, chopped finely

1 cup sliced carrots

⅔ cup stout

2 tbsp melted butter

2

4

3

1 Remove the skin from the chicken quarters, if preferred.

2 Arrange a layer of potato slices in the bottom of a wide casserole. Season with salt and pepper, then add the thyme, rosemary, and bay leaves.

3 Top with the chicken quarters, then sprinkle with the diced bacon, onion, and carrots. Season well and arrange the remaining potato slices on top, overlapping slightly.

4 Pour over the stout, brush the potatoes with the melted butter, and cover with a lid.

5 Bake in a preheated oven, 300°F, for about 2 hours, uncovering for the last 30 minutes to allow the potatoes to brown. Serve hot.

cooks tip

Serve the hotch-potch with dumplings for a truly hearty meal.

variation

This dish is also delicious with stewing lamb, cut into chunks. You can add different vegetables depending on what is in season—try leeks and swedes for a slightly sweeter flavor.

chicken madeira french-style

Madeira is a fortified wine which can be used in both sweet and savory dishes. Here it adds a rich, full flavor to the casserole.

Serves 8

2 tbsp butter

20 baby onions

1½ cups carrots, sliced

1½ cups bacon, chopped

3 cups white mushrooms

1 chicken, weighing about 3 lb 5 oz

1⅛ cups white wine

¼ cup seasoned flour

1⅛ cups chicken bouillon

salt and pepper

bouquet garni

⅔ cup Madeira wine

mashed potato or pasta, to serve

1 Heat the butter in a large skillet and sauté the onions, carrots, bacon and mushrooms for 3 minutes, stirring frequently. Transfer to a large casserole dish.

2 Add the chicken to the skillet and brown all over. Transfer to the casserole dish with the vegetables and bacon.

2

4

3 Add the white wine and cook until the wine is nearly completely reduced.

4 Sprinkle with the seasoned flour, stirring to avoid lumps from forming.

5 Add the chicken bouillon, salt and pepper to taste and the bouquet garni. Cover and cook the casserole for 2 hours. About 30 minutes before the end of cooking time, add the Madeira wine and continue cooking uncovered.

6 Carve the chicken and serve with mashed potato or pasta.

cook's tip

You can add any combination of herbs to this recipe—chervil is a popular herb in French cuisine, but add it at the end of cooking so that its delicate flavour is not lost. Other herbs which work well with chicken are parsley and tarragon.

3

californian chicken

It is better if you have time to bone the chicken completely, or use chicken breast after removing all the fat and skin.

Serves 4-6

1½ cups all-purpose flour

1 tsp paprika

1 tsp freeze-dried Italian seasoning

1 tsp freeze-dried tarragon

1 tsp rosemary, finely crushed

2 eggs, beaten

½ cup milk

1 chicken, weighing about 4 lb, jointed

seasoned flour

⅔ cup rapeseed oil

2 bananas, quartered

1 apple, cut into rings,

12 oz can corn and peppers, drained

oil for sautéing

salt and pepper

bunch of watercress

peppercorn or horseradish sauce, to serve

1 Mix together the flour, spices, herbs, and a pinch of salt in a large bowl. Make a well in the center and add the eggs.

2 Blend and slowly add the milk, whisking until very smooth.

3 Coat the chicken pieces with seasoned flour and dip the chicken pieces into the batter mix.

4 Heat the oil in a large skillet. Add the chicken and sauté for about 3 minutes or until lightly browned all over. Place the chicken pieces on a non-stick cookie sheet.

5 Batter the bananas and apple rings and sauté for 2 minutes.

6 Finally toss the corn and peppers into the leftover batter.

7 Heat a little oil in a skillet. Drop in spoonfuls of the corn mixture to make flat patty cakes. Cook for 4 minutes on each side. Keep warm with the apple and banana fritters.

8 Bake the chicken in a preheated oven, 400°F, for about 25 minutes until the chicken is tender and golden brown.

9 Arrange the chicken, corn fritters, and the apple and banana fritters, on a bed of fresh watercress. Serve with a peppercorn or horseradish sauce.

1

3

7

country chicken bake

This economical bake is a complete meal—its crusty, herb-flavored French bread topping mops up the tasty juices, and means there's no need to serve potatoes or rice separately.

Serves 4

2 tbsp sunflower oil

4 chicken quarters

16 small whole onions, peeled

3 stalks celery, sliced

14 oz can red kidney beans

4 medium tomatoes, quartered

scant 1 cup dry cider or bouillon

4 tbsp chopped fresh parsley

1 tsp paprika

salt and pepper4 tbsp butter

12 slices French bread

cook's tip

Add a crushed garlic clove to the parsley butter for extra flavour.

variation

For a more unusual Italian-tasting dish, replace the garlic and parsley bread topping with the pesto-covered toasts.

2

2

1 Heat the oil in a flameproof casserole and sauté the chicken quarters two at a time until golden. Using a draining spoon, remove the chicken from the pan and set aside until required.

2 Add the onions and sauté, turning occasionally, until golden brown. Add the celery and sauté for 2–3 minutes. Return the chicken to the pan, then stir in the beans, tomatoes, cider, half the parsley, salt, and pepper. Sprinkle with the paprika.

3 Cover and cook in a preheated oven, 400°F, for 20–25 minutes, until the chicken juices run clear when pierced with a skewer.

4

4 Mix the remaining parsley with the butter and spread evenly over the French bread.

5 Uncover the casserole, arrange the bread slices so that they are overlapping on top and bake for a further 10–12 minutes, until golden and crisp.

cheddar-baked chicken

Cheese and mustard, and a simple, crispy coating, make a delicious combination for this healthy dish.

Serves 4

1 tbsp milk

2 tbsp prepared English mustard

1 cup grated mature hard cheese

3 tbsp all-purpose flour

2 tbsp chopped fresh chives

4 skinless, boneless chicken breasts

1

3

cook's tip

There are several varieties of mustard available. For a sharper flavor try French varieties—Meaux mustard has a grainy texture with a warm, spicy flavor while Dijon mustard is medium-hot and tangy.

2

cook's tip

It is a good idea to freeze herbs as they retain their color, flavor, and nutrients very well. Chives are particularly suitable for freezing—store them in labeled plastic bags and shake them dry before use. Dried chives are not an adequate substitute for fresh.

1 Mix together the milk and mustard in a bowl. In another bowl, combine the cheese, flour, and chives.

2 Dip the chicken into the milk and mustard mixture, brushing to coat evenly.

3 Dip the chicken breasts into the cheese mixture, pressing to coat evenly. Place on a cookie sheet and spoon any spare cheese coating over the top.

4 Bake in a preheated oven, 400°F, for 30–35 minutes, or until golden brown and the juices run clear, not pink, when pierced with a skewer. Serve the chicken hot, with jacket potatoes and fresh vegetables, or serve cold, with a crisp salad.

feta chicken with mountain herbs

Chicken goes well with most savory herbs, especially during the summer, when fresh herbs are at their best. This combination makes a good partner for tangy feta cheese and sun-ripened tomatoes.

Serves 4

8 skinless, boneless chicken thighs

2 tbsp each chopped fresh thyme, rosemary
   and oregano

4½ oz feta cheese

1 tbsp milk

2 tbsp all-purpose flour

salt and pepper

thyme, rosemary, and oregano, to garnish

TOMATO SAUCE

1 medium onion, roughly chopped

1 garlic clove, crushed

1 tbsp olive oil

4 medium plum tomatoes, quartered

sprig each of thyme, rosemary, and oregano

2

3

6

1 Spread out the chicken thighs, smooth side downward.

2 Divide the herbs among the chicken thighs, then cut the cheese into eight sticks. Place one stick of cheese in the center of each chicken thigh. Season well, then roll up to enclose the cheese.

3 Place the rolls in an ovenproof dish, brush with milk, and dust with flour to coat.

4 Bake in a preheated oven, 375°F, for 25–30 minutes, or until golden brown. The juices should run clear and not pink when the chicken is pierced with a skewer in the thickest part.

5 To make the sauce, cook the onion and garlic in the olive oil, stirring, until softened and starting to brown.

6 Add the tomatoes, reduce the heat, cover, and simmer for 15–20 minutes or until soft.

7 Add the herbs, then transfer to a food processor and blend to a paste. Press through a strainer to make a smooth, rich sauce. Season and serve the sauce with the chicken, garnished with herbs.

chicken with creamy zucchini & lime stuffing

A cheesy stuffing is tucked under the breast skin of the chicken to give added flavor and moistness to the meat.

Serves 6

1 chicken, weighing 5 lb

oil for brushing

1¼ cups zucchini

2 tbsp butter

juice of 1 lime

STUFFING

½ cup zucchini

¾ cup medium-fat soft cheese

finely grated rind of 1 lime

2 tbsp fresh bread crumbs

salt and pepper

cook's tip

For quicker cooking, finely grate the zucchini rather than cutting them into strips.

2

3

5

1 To make the stuffing, trim and coarsely grate the zucchini and mix with the cheese, lime peel, bread crumbs, salt, and pepper.

2 Carefully case the skin away from the breast of the chicken.

3 Push the stuffing under the skin with your fingers, to cover the breast evenly.

4 Place the chicken in a baking pan, brush with oil, and roast in a preheated oven, 375°F, for 20 minutes per 1 lb 2 oz plus 20 minutes, or until the juices run clear when the thickest part of the chicken is pierced with a skewer.

5 Meanwhile, trim the remaining zucchini and cut into long, thin strips with a potato peeler or sharp knife. Sauté in the butter and lime juice until just tender, then serve with the chicken.

pollo catalan

The Catalan region of Spain is famous for its wonderful combinations of meat with fruit. In this recipe, peaches lend a touch of sweetness and pine nuts, cinnamon, and sherry add an unusual twist.

Serves 6

1 cup fresh brown bread crumbs

½ cup pine nuts

1 small egg, beaten

4 tbsp chopped fresh thyme
  or 1 tbsp dried thyme

4 fresh peaches or 8 canned peach halves

salt and pepper

1 chicken, weighing about 5½ lb

1 tsp ground cinnamon

¾ cup Amontillado sherry

4 tbsp heavy cream

1

3

4

cook's tip

Canned apricot halves in natural juice make an easy pantry alternative.

1 Combine the bread crumbs with ¼ cup pine nuts, the egg, and the thyme.

2 Halve and stone the peaches, removing the skin if necessary. Dice one peach into small pieces and stir into the bread crumb mixture. Season well. Spoon the stuffing into the neck cavity of the chicken, securing the skin firmly over it.

3 Place the chicken in a roasting pan. Sprinkle the cinnamon over the skin.

4 Cover loosely with foil and roast in a preheated oven, 375°F, for 1 hour, basting occasionally.

5 Remove the foil and spoon the sherry over the chicken. Cook for a further 30 minutes, basting with the sherry, until the juices run clear when the chicken is pierced in the thickest part with a skewer.

6 Sprinkle the remaining pine nuts over the remaining peach halves and place in an ovenproof dish in the oven for the final 10 minutes of cooking time.

7 Lift the chicken on to a serving plate and arrange the peach halves around it. Skim any fat from the juices, stir in the cream, and heat gently. Serve with the chicken.

whiskey roast chicken

An unusual change from a plain roast, with a distinctly warming Scottish flavor and a delicious oatmeal stuffing.

Serves 6

1 chicken, weighing 4 lb 8 oz

oil, for brushing

1 tbsp heather honey

2 tbsp Scotch whiskey

2 tbsp all-purpose flour

1¼ cups chicken bouillon

STUFFING

1 medium onion, finely chopped

1 stalk celery, sliced thinly

1 tbsp butter or sunflower oil

1 tsp dried thyme

4 tbsp porridge oats

4 tbsp chicken bouillon

salt and pepper

a green vegetable and sautéed potatoes,
    to serve

2

4

4 Mix the heather honey with 1 tablespoon whiskey and brush the mixture over the chicken. Return to the oven for a further 20 minutes, or until the chicken is golden brown and the juices run clear when the chicken is pierced through the thickest part with a skewer.

5 Lift the chicken on to a serving plate. Skim the fat from the juices then stir in the flour. Stir over a moderate heat until the mixture starts to bubble, then gradually add the bouillon and remaining whiskey.

6 Bring to the boil, stirring, simmer for 1 minute, and serve the chicken with the sauce, a green vegetable, and sautéed potatoes.

5

1 To make the stuffing, sauté the onion and celery in the butter or oil, stirring over a medium heat until softened.

2 Remove from the heat and stir in the thyme, oats, bouillon, salt, and pepper.

3 Stuff the neck end of the chicken with the mixture and tuck the neck flap under. Place in a roasting pan, brush lightly with oil, and roast in a preheated oven, 375°F, for about 1 hour.

boned chicken with parmesan

It's really very easy to bone a whole chicken, but if you prefer, you can ask a friendly butcher to do this for you.

Serves 6

1 chicken, weighing about 5 lb

8 slices Mortadella or salami

2 cups fresh white or brown bread crumbs

1 cup freshly grated Parmesan cheese

2 garlic cloves, crushed

6 tbsp chopped fresh basil or parsley

pepper

1 egg, beaten

fresh spring vegetables, to serve

variation

Replace the Mortadella with slices of bacon, if preferred.

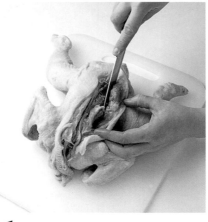

1

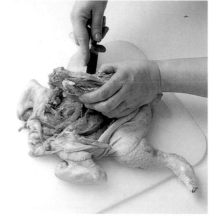

2

1 Bone the chicken, keeping the skin intact. Dislocate each leg by breaking it at the thigh joint. Cut down each side of the backbone, taking care not to pierce the breast skin.

2 Pull the backbone clear of the flesh and discard. Remove the ribs, severing any attached flesh with a sharp knife.

3 Scrape the flesh from each leg and cut away the bone at the joint with a knife or shears.

4 Use the bones for bouillon. Lay out the boned chicken on a board, skin side down. Arrange the Mortadella slices over the chicken, overlapping slightly.

5 Put the bread crumbs, Parmesan, garlic, and basil or parsley in a bowl. Season well with pepper and mix. Stir in the beaten egg to bind the mixture together. Pile the mixture down the middle of the boned chicken, roll the meat around it, and tie securely with fine cotton string.

6 Place in a roasting dish and brush lightly with olive oil. Roast in a preheated oven at 400°F for 1½ hours or until the juices run clear when pierced.

7 Serve hot or cold, in slices, with fresh spring vegetables.

3

honey & mustard-baked chicken

Chicken portions are brushed with a classic combination of honey and mustard then a crunchy coating of poppy seeds is added.

1

Serves 4-6

8 chicken portions

4 tbsp butter, melted

4 tbsp mild mustard

4 tbsp honey

2 tbsp lemon juice

1 tsp paprika

salt and pepper

3 tbsp poppy seeds

tomato and corn salad, to serve (optional)

1 Place the chicken pieces, skinless side down, on a large cookie sheet.

2 Place all the ingredients except the poppy seeds into a large bowl and blend together thoroughly.

3 Brush the mixture over the chicken portions.

4 Bake in the center of a preheated oven, 400°F, for 15 minutes.

5 Carefully turn over the chicken pieces and coat the top side of the chicken with the remaining honey and mustard mixture.

3

5

6 Sprinkle the chicken with poppy seeds and return to the oven for a further 15 minutes.

7 Arrange the chicken on a serving dish, pour over the cooking juices, and serve with a tomato and corn salad, if wished.

cook's tip

Mexican rice makes an excellent accompaniment to this dish: boil the rice for 10 minutes, drain, then sauté for 5 minutes. Add chopped onions, garlic, tomatoes, carrots, and chili, and cook for 1 minute before adding bouillon. Bring to the boil, cover and simmer for 20 minutes, adding more bouillon if necessary. Add peas 5 minutes before the end of the cooking time.

chicken with york ham & stilton

Beet is one of the most underrated vegetables, adding flavor and color to numerous dishes. Tender young beet are used in this recipe.

Serves 4

4 chicken suprêmes

8 fresh sage leaves

8 thin slices of York ham

2 cups Stilton cheese, cut into 8 slices

8 slices rindless streaky bacon

⅔ cup chicken bouillon

2 tbsp port

24 shallots

1 lb 2 oz baby beet, cooked

1 tbsp cornstarch, blended with a little port

salt and pepper

1 Cut a long slit horizontally along each chicken breast to make a pocket.

2 Insert 2 sage leaves into each pocket and season lightly.

3 Wrap each slice of ham around a slice of cheese and place 2 into each chicken pocket. Carefully wrap enough bacon around each breast to completely cover the pockets containing the ham and the cheese.

4 Place the breasts in an ovenproof casserole dish and pour over the bouillon and port.

5 Add the shallots, cover with a lid or cooking foil and braise in a preheated oven 375°F, for about 40 minutes.

6 Carefully place each breast on to a cutting board and slice through them to create a fan effect. Serve them on a warm serving dish with the shallots and beet.

7 Put the juices from the casserole into a saucepan and bring to the boil, remove from the heat, and add the cornflour paste. Gently simmer and cook the sauce for 2 minutes, then pour over the shallots and beet.

variation

Use any blue-veined cheese instead of the Stilton, if you prefer. Try Gorgonzola or Roquefort.

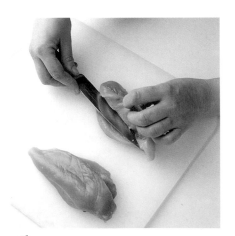

1

3

3

gardener's chicken

Any combination of small, young vegetables can be roasted with the chicken, such as zucchini, leeks, and onions.

Serves 4

4 cups parsnips, peeled and chopped

¾ cup carrots, peeled and chopped

½ cup fresh bread crumbs

¼ tsp grated nutmeg

1 tbsp chopped fresh parsley

salt and pepper

3 lb 5 oz chicken

bunch parsley

½ onion

2 tbsp butter, softened

4 tbsp olive oil

1 lb 2 oz new potatoes, scrubbed

1 lb 2 oz baby carrots, washed and trimmed

chopped fresh parsley, to garnish

1 To make the stuffing, put the parsnips and carrots into a pan, half cover with water, and bring to the boil. Cover the pan and simmer until tender. Drain well then paste in a blender or food processor. Transfer the paste to a bowl and leave to cool.

2 Mix in the bread crumbs, nutmeg, and parsley and season with salt and pepper.

3 Put the stuffing into the neck end of the chicken and push a little under the skin over the breast meat. Secure the flap of skin with a small metal skewer or toothpick.

4 Place the bunch of parsley and onion inside the cavity of the chicken, then place the chicken in a large roasting pan.

5 Spread the butter over the skin and season with salt and pepper, cover with foil, and place in a preheated oven, 375°F, for 30 minutes.

2

3

4

6 Meanwhile, heat the oil in a skillet and lightly brown the potatoes.

7 Transfer the potatoes to the roasting pan and add the baby carrots. Baste the chicken and continue to cook for a further hour, basting the chicken and vegetables after 30 minutes. Remove the foil for the last 20 minutes to allow the skin to crisp. Garnish the vegetables with chopped parsley and serve.

golden chicken with mango & cranberries

This recipe, which uses a partly-boned chicken is easy to slice and serve. If you prefer, stuff in the traditional way at the neck end, and cook any remaining stuffing separately.

Serves 4

1 chicken, weighing about 5 lb

6 slices smoked bacon

STUFFING

1 ripe mango, diced

¼ cup fresh or frozen cranberries

2 cups bread crumbs

½ tsp ground mace

1 egg, beaten

salt and pepper

GLAZE

½ tsp ground turmeric

2 tsp honey

2 tsp sunflower oil

1 To part-bone the chicken, dislocate the legs and place the chicken breast-side downward. Cut a straight line through the skin along the ridge of the back. Scrape the meat down from the bone on both sides.

2 When you reach the point where the legs and wings join the body, cut through the joints. Work around the ribcage until the carcass can be lifted away.

3 Make six bacon rolls. For the stuffing, mix the mango with the cranberries, bread crumbs, and mace, then bind with egg. Season.

4 Place the chicken, skin-side down, and spoon over half the stuffing.

Arrange the bacon rolls down the center, then top with the remaining stuffing. Fold the skin over and tie with string. Turn the chicken over, truss the legs, and tuck the wings underneath. Place in a roasting pan. To make the glaze, mix the turmeric, honey, and oil, and brush over the skin.

5 Roast in a preheated oven, 375°F, for 1½–2 hours or until the juices run clear, not pink, when the chicken is pierced with a skewer. When the chicken starts to brown, cover loosely with foil to prevent overbrowning. Serve the chicken hot with vegetables.

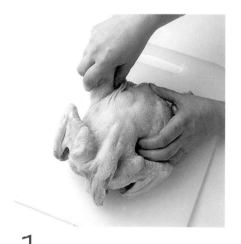

1

1

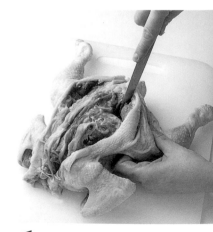

1

pot-roast orange & sesame chicken

This colorful, nutritious pot-roast could be served for a family meal or for a special dinner. Add more vegetables if you're feeding a crowd—if your roasting pot is large enough!

Serves 4

2 tbsp sunflower oil

1 chicken, weighing about 3 lb 5 oz

2 large oranges

2 small onions, quartered

2 cups small whole carrots or thin carrots,
   cut into 2 inch pieces

⅔ cup orange juice

2 tbsp brandy

2 tbsp sesame seeds

1 tbsp cornstarch

salt and pepper

variation

Use lemons instead of oranges
for a sharper citrus flavor
and place a sprig of fresh
thyme in the chicken cavity
with the lemon half as they
are a good flavor combination.

1 Heat the oil in a large flameproof casserole and sauté the chicken, turning occasionally until evenly browned.

2 Cut one orange in half and place half inside the chicken cavity. Place the chicken in a large, deep casserole. Arrange the onions and carrots around the chicken.

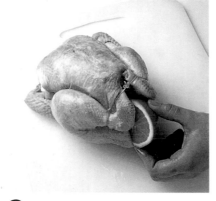

2

3

4

3 Season well and pour over the orange juice.

4 Cut the remaining oranges into thin wedges and tuck around the chicken in the casserole, among the vegetables.

5 Cover and cook in a preheated oven, 350°F, for about 1½ hours, or until there is no trace of pink in the chicken juices when pierced, and the vegetables are tender. Remove the lid and sprinkle with the brandy and sesame seeds, and return to the oven for 10 minutes.

6 To serve, lift the chicken on to a large platter. Place the vegetables around the chicken. Skim any excess fat from the juices. Blend the cornflour with 1 tablespoon cold water, stir into the juices, and bring to the boil, stirring all the time. Adjust the seasoning to taste, then serve the sauce with the chicken.

festive apple chicken

The richly flavored stuffing in this recipe is cooked under the breast skin of the chicken, so not only is all the flavor sealed in, but the chicken stays really moist and succulent during cooking.

Serves 6

1 chicken, weighing 4 lb

oil, for brushing

2 eating apples

1 tbsp butter

1 tbsp redcurrant jelly

mixed vegetables, to serve

STUFFING

1 tbsp butter

1 small onion, chopped finely

2 oz mushrooms, chopped finely

2 oz smoked ham, chopped finely

½ cup fresh bread crumbs

1 tbsp chopped fresh parsley

1 crisp eating apple

1 tbsp lemon juice

salt and pepper

2 Core the apple, leaving the skin on, and grate coarsely. Add the stuffing mixture to the apple with the lemon juice. Season to taste.

3 Loosen the breast skin of the chicken and carefully spoon the stuffing mixture under it, smoothing the skin over evenly with your hands.

4 Place the chicken in a roasting pan and brush lightly with oil.

5 Roast the chicken in a preheated oven, 375°F, for 25 minutes per 1 lb plus 25 minutes, or until there is no trace of pink in the juices when the chicken is pierced through the thickest part with a skewer. If the breast starts to brown too much, cover the chicken with foil.

4

6

1 To make the stuffing, melt the butter and sauté the onion gently, stirring until softened but not browned. Stir in the mushrooms and cook for 2–3 minutes. Remove from the heat and stir in the ham, bread crumbs, and the chopped parsley.

2

6 Core and slice the remaining apples and sauté in the butter until golden. Stir in the redcurrant jelly and warm through until melted. Garnish the chicken with the apple slices and serve with mixed vegetables.

chicken with marmalade stuffing

Marmalade lovers will enjoy this festive recipe. You can use any favorite marmalade, such as lemon or grapefruit.

Serves 6

1 chicken, weighing about 5 lb

bay leaves

STUFFING

1 stalk celery, chopped finely

1 small onion, chopped finely

1 tbsp sunflower oil

2 cups fresh whole wheat bread crumbs

4 tbsp marmalade

2 tbsp chopped fresh parsley

1 egg, beaten

salt and pepper

SAUCE

2 tsp cornstarch

2 tbsp orange juice

3 tbsp marmalade

⅔ cup chicken bouillon

1 medium orange

2 tbsp brandy

new potatoes, to serve

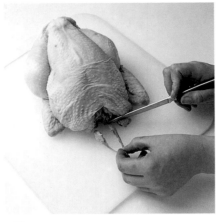

1

1 Lift the neck flap of the chicken and remove the wishbone using a small, sharp knife. Place a sprig of bay leaves inside the body cavity.

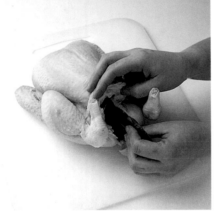

1

2 For the stuffing, sauté the celery and onion in the oil to soften. Add the bread crumbs, 3 tablespoons of marmalade, parsley, and egg. Season and use to stuff the neck cavity of the chicken. Any extra stuffing may be cooked separately.

3 Place the chicken in a roasting pan and brush lightly with oil. Roast in a preheated oven, 375°F, for 20 minutes per 1 lb 2 oz plus 20 minutes or until the juices run clear when the chicken is pierced in the thickest part with a skewer. Remove from the oven and glaze with the remaining marmalade.

4

4 Meanwhile, to make the sauce, blend the cornstarch in a pan with the orange juice, then add the marmalade and chicken bouillon. Heat gently, stirring, until thickened and smooth. Remove from the heat. Cut the segments from the orange, discarding all white pith and membrane. Just before serving, add the orange segments and brandy to the sauce and bring to the boil.

5 Serve the chicken with the orange sauce, any extra stuffing, and new potatoes.

mediterranean-style sunday roast

A roast that is full of Mediterranean flavor. A mixture of feta cheese, rosemary, and sun-dried tomatoes is stuffed under the chicken skin, then roasted with garlic, new potatoes, and vegetables.

Serves 6

5 lb 8 oz chicken

sprigs of fresh rosemary

¾ cup feta cheese, coarsely grated

2 tbsp sun-dried tomato paste

4 tbsp butter, softened

pepper

1 bulb garlic

2 lb 4 oz new potatoes, halved if large

1 each red, green, and yellow bell pepper,
   cut into chunks

3 zucchini, sliced thinly

2 tbsp olive oil

2 tbsp all-purpose flour

2½ cups chicken bouillon

2

4

3

1 Rinse the chicken inside and out with cold water and drain well. Carefully cut between the skin and the top of the breast meat using a small pointed knife. Slide a finger into the slit and carefully enlarge it to form a pocket. Continue until the skin is completely lifted away from both breasts and the top of the legs.

2 Chop the leaves from 3 rosemary stems. Mix with the feta, sun-dried tomato paste, butter, and pepper then spoon under the skin. Put the chicken in a large roasting pan, cover with foil, and cook in a preheated oven, 375°F, for 20 minutes per 1 lb 2 oz plus 20 minutes.

3 Break the garlic bulb into cloves but do not peel. Add the vegetables to the chicken after 40 minutes.

4 Drizzle with oil, tuck in a few stems of rosemary, and season well. Cook for the remaining time, removing the foil for the last 40 minutes of cooking to brown the chicken.

5 Transfer the chicken to a serving platter. Place some of the vegetables around the chicken and transfer the remainder to a warmed serving dish. Pour the fat out of the roasting pan and stir the flour into the remaining pan juices. Cook for 2 minutes then gradually stir in the bouillon. Bring to the boil, stirring until thickened. Strain into a sauce boat and serve with the chicken.

honeyed citrus chicken

This fat-free recipe is great for summer entertaining served simply with a green salad and new potatoes. If you cut the chicken in half and press it flat, you can roast it in under an hour.

Serves 4

4 lb 8 oz chicken

salt and pepper

2 oranges, cut into wedges

tarragon sprigs, to garnish

MARINADE

1¼ cups orange juice

3 tbsp cider vinegar

3 tbsp honey

2 tbsp chopped fresh tarragon

SAUCE

handful of tarragon sprigs, chopped

1 cup fat-free fromage blanc

2 tbsp orange juice

1 tsp honey

1/2 cup stuffed olives, chopped

1

2

1 Put the chicken on a chopping
board with the breast downward.
Cut through the bottom part of the
carcass using poultry shears or heavy
kitchen scissors, making sure not to cut
right through to the breast bone below.

2 Rinse the chicken with cold water,
drain, and place on a board with the
skin side uppermost. Press the chicken
flat, then cut off the leg ends.

3 Thread two long wooden skewers
through the bird to keep it flat.
Season the skin.

4 Put all the marinade ingredients in a
shallow, nonmetallic dish. Mix, then
add the chicken. Cover and chill for 4
hours, turning the chicken several times.

5 To make the sauce, mix all the
ingredients and season. Spoon into
a serving dish, cover, and chill.

6 Transfer the chicken and marinade
to a roasting pan, open out the
chicken, and place skin-side downward.
Tuck the orange wedges around the
chicken and roast in a preheated oven,
400°F, for 25 minutes. Turn the chicken
over and roast for another 20–30
minutes. Baste until the chicken is
browned and the juices run clear when
pierced with a skewer. Garnish with
tarragon and serve with the sauce.

3

chicken with bacon & dripping

Chicken suprêmes have a little bit of the wing bone remaining which makes them easy to pick up and eat. In this recipe, a tart, fruity sauce perfectly complements the chicken and dripping triangles.

Serves 8

4 tbsp butter

juice of 1 lemon

1 cup redcurrants or cranberries

1–2 tbsp muscovado sugar

salt and pepper

8 chicken suprêmes or breasts

16 slices of streaky bacon

thyme

4 tbsp beef drippings

4 slices of bread, cut into triangles

1

2

1 Heat the butter in a pan, add the lemon juice, redcurrants or cranberries, muscovado sugar, and salt and pepper to taste. Cook for 1 minute and allow to cool until required.

2 Meanwhile, season the chicken with salt and pepper. Wrap 2 slices of streaky bacon around each breast and sprinkle with thyme.

3 Wrap each breast in a piece of lightly greased foil and place in a roasting pan. Roast in a preheated oven, 400°F, for 15 minutes. Remove the foil and roast for another 10 minutes.

4

4 Heat the drippings in a skillet, add the bread triangles and sauté on both sides until golden brown.

5 Arrange the triangles on a large serving plate and top each with a chicken breast. Serve with a spoonful of the fruit sauce.

cook's tip

You can use either chopped fresh thyme or dried thyme in this recipe, but remember that dried herbs have a stronger flavor so you only need half the quantity compared to fresh herbs.

roast chicken with cilantro & garlic

This recipe for chicken is coated with a fresh-flavored marinade then roasted. Try serving it with rice, yogurt, and salad.

Serves 4-6

3 sprigs fresh cilantro, chopped

4 garlic cloves

½ tsp salt

pepper

4 tbsp lemon juice

4 tbsp olive oil

1 large chicken

sprig of fresh parsley, to garnish

boiled potatoes and carrots, to serve

1

2

1 Place the chopped cilantro, garlic, salt, 1 teaspoon pepper, lemon juice, and olive oil in a pestle and mortar and pound together or blend in a food processor. Chill for 4 hours to allow the flavors to develop.

2 Place the chicken in a roasting pan. Coat generously with the cilantro and garlic mixture.

3

3 Sprinkle with extra pepper and roast in a preheated oven, 375°F, on a low shelf for 1½ hours, basting every 20 minutes with the coriander mixture. If the chicken starts to turn brown, cover with foil. Garnish with parsley and serve with the boiled potatoes and carrots.

cook's tip

For pounding small quantities it is best to use a pestle and mortar so as little as possible of the mixture is left in the container.

variation

Any fresh herb can be used in this recipe instead of the cilantro. Tarragon or thyme are a good combination with chicken.

poussin with dried fruits

Baby chickens are ideal for a one or two portion meal, and cook very easily and quickly for a special dinner. If you're cooking for one, a microwave makes cooking even quicker and more convenient.

Serves 2

¾ cup dried apples, peaches, and prunes

½ cup boiling water

2 baby chickens

⅓ cup walnut halves

1 tbsp honey

1 tsp ground allspice

1 tbsp walnut oil

salt and pepper

fresh vegetables and new potatoes, to serve

1 Place the dried fruits in a bowl, cover with the boiling water, and leave to stand for about 30 minutes.

2 Cut the chickens in half down the breastbone using a sharp knife, or leave them whole, if you prefer.

3 Mix the fruit and any juices remaining in the bowl with the walnut halves, honey, and ground allspice and divide the mixture between two small roasting bags or squares of foil.

4 Brush the chickens with walnut oil and sprinkle with salt and pepper then place on top of the fruits.

5 Close the roasting bags or fold the foil over to enclose the chickens and bake on a cookie sheet in a preheated oven, 375°F, for 25–30 minutes or until the juices run clear and not pink when the chicken is pierced in the thickest part with a skewer. To cook in a microwave, use microwave roasting bags and cook on high power for 6–7 minutes.

6 Serve hot with fresh vegetables and new potatoes.

cook's tip

Alternative dried fruits that can be used in this recipe are cherries, mangoes, or papaya.

1

3

5

springtime roast chicken

Baby chickens are simple to prepare, take about 30 minutes to roast and can be easily cut in half lengthways with a sharp knife. One baby chicken makes a substantial serving for each person.

5

Serves 4

5 tbsp fresh brown bread crumbs

½ cup fromage blanc or unsweetened yogurt

5 tbsp chopped fresh parsley

5 tbsp chopped fresh chives

salt and pepper

4 baby chickens

1 tbsp sunflower oil

1½ lb young spring vegetables such as
carrots, zucchini, sugar snap peas, corn,
and turnips, cut into small chunks

½ cup boiling chicken bouillon

2 tsp cornstarch

⅔ cup dry white wine

1 In a bowl, mix together the bread crumbs, one-third of the fromage blanc or yogurt and 2 tablespoons each of parsley and chives. Season well with salt and pepper then spoon into the neck ends of the baby chickens. Place the chickens on a rack in a roasting pan, brush with oil, and season well.

2

3

2 Roast in a preheated oven, 425°F, for 30–35 minutes or until the juices run clear, not pink, when the chickens are pierced with a skewer.

3 Place the vegetables in a shallow ovenproof dish in one layer and add half the remaining herbs with the chicken bouillon. Cover and bake for 25–30 minutes until tender. Strain the vegetables, reserving the cooking juices, and keep warm.

4 Lift the chickens on to a serving plate and skim any fat from the juices in the pan. Add the reserved vegetable juices.

5 Blend the cornstarch with the wine and whisk into the sauce with the remaining fromage blanc or yogurt. Whisk until boiling, then add the remaining herbs. Season to taste. Spoon the sauce over the chickens and serve with the vegetables.

There is nothing more delicious than the juicy flesh and charred skin of chicken that has been grilled over an open fire—after marinating in a flavorful mixture of oil and herbs or spices. Try an Asian-style mixture of yogurt and aromatic spices, or soy sauce, sesame oil,

and fresh gingerroot. There are some unusual flavors and innovative tastes, including Skewered Chicken with Bramble Sauce, and Skewered Chicken Spirals, which are attractive whirls of chicken, bacon, and basil. Baby chickens, flavored with lemon and tarragon in this section, are perfect for broiling or barbecuing. There is also a recipe for Broiled Chicken & Vegetable Salad which combines chicken breasts with a selection of broiled vegetables including zucchini, eggplant, and bell pepper drizzled with olive oil and served with crusty bread to soak up the delicious juices.

barbecues
& broils

chicken tikka skewers

Traditionally, chicken tikka is cooked in a clay tandoori oven, but it works well grilled over hot coals on the barbecue too.

Makes 6

4 chicken breasts, skinned and boned

½ tsp salt

4 tbsp lemon or lime juice

oil or melted butter for brushing

MARINADE

⅔ cup unsweetened yogurt

2 cloves garlic, finely chopped

1 inch piece gingerroot, peeled and grated

1 tsp ground cumin

1 tsp chili powder

½ tsp ground coriander

½ tsp ground turmeric

SAUCE

⅔ cup unsweetened yogurt

1 tsp mint sauce

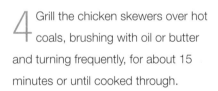

1 Cut the chicken into 1 inch cubes. Sprinkle with the salt and the lemon or lime juice and leave to stand for about 10 minutes.

2 To make the marinade, combine the yogurt, garlic, gingerroot, and ground spices together in a small bowl until well mixed.

3 Thread the cubes of chicken on to skewers. Brush the marinade over the chicken. Cover and leave to marinate in the refrigerator for at least 2 hours, preferably overnight.

4 Grill the chicken skewers over hot coals, brushing with oil or butter and turning frequently, for about 15 minutes or until cooked through.

5 Meanwhile, combine the yogurt and mint to make the sauce. Serve the chicken skewers with the mint and yogurt sauce.

variation

Use the marinade to coat chicken portions, such as drumsticks, rather than cubes of chicken, if you prefer. Grill over medium hot coals for 30–40 minutes, until the juices run clear when the chicken is pierced with a skewer.

maryland chicken kabobs

A barbecue variation of the traditional dish, Chicken Maryland. Serve with corn and a tasty mango relish.

Serves 4

3 chicken thighs, skinned and boned

1 tbsp white wine vinegar

1 tbsp lemon juice

1 tbsp golden syrup or honey

3 tbsp olive oil

1 clove garlic, finely chopped

salt and pepper

4 slices rindless, smoked, streaky bacon

2 bananas

cooked corn and mango relish, to serve

variation

For a quick Maryland-style dish, omit the marinating time and cook the chicken thighs over hot coals for about 20 minutes, basting with the marinade. Grill the bananas in their skins alongside the chicken. Serve the bananas split open with a teaspoon of mango relish.

3

4

1 Cut the chicken into bite-size pieces. Combine the vinegar, lemon juice, syrup or honey, oil, garlic, and salt and pepper to taste in a large bowl. Add the chicken to the marinade and toss until the chicken is well coated. Cover and leave to marinate for 1–2 hours.

2 Stretch the bacon slices with the back of a knife and then cut each bacon rasher in half. Cut the bananas into 1 inch lengths and brush them with lemon juice to prevent any discoloration.

3 Wrap a piece of bacon around each piece of banana.

4 Remove the chicken from the marinade, reserving the marinade for basting. Thread the chicken pieces and the bacon and banana rolls alternately on to skewers.

5

5 Barbecue the kabobs over hot coals for 8–10 minutes until the chicken is completely cooked. Baste the kabobs with the marinade and turn the skewers frequently.

6 Serve with corn and mango relish.

chicken skewers with red bell pepper sauce

These kabobs are rather special and are well worth the extra effort needed to prepare them.

Serves 4

3 chicken breasts, skinned and boned

6 tbsp olive oil

4 tbsp lemon juice

½ small onion, grated

1 tbsp fresh, chopped sage

8 tbsp sage and onion stuffing mix

6 tbsp boiling water

2 green bell peppers, seeded

SAUCE

1 tbsp olive oil

1 red bell pepper, seeded and chopped finely

1 small onion, chopped finely

pinch sugar

7½ oz can chopped tomatoes

2

4

1 Cut the chicken into evenly sized pieces.

2 Mix the oil, lemon juice grated onion, and sage, and pour the mixture into a plastic bag. Add the chicken, seal the bag, and shake to coat the chicken. Leave to marinate for at least 30 minutes, shaking the bag occasionally.

3 Place the stuffing mix in a bowl and add a little boiling water, stirring to mix well.

4 Cut each bell pepper into 6 strips, then blanch them in boiling water for 3–4 minutes until softened. Drain, refresh under running water, and drain again.

5 Form about 1 teaspoon of the stuffing mixture into a ball and roll it up in a strip of bell pepper. Repeat for the remaining stuffing mixture and bell pepper strips. Thread 3 bell pepper rolls on to each skewer alternatively with pieces of chicken. Leave to chill.

6 To make the sauce, heat the oil in a small pan and sauté the red bell pepper and onion for 5 minutes. Add the sugar and tomatoes and simmer for about 5 minutes. Set aside and keep warm.

7 Grill the skewers on an oiled rack over hot coals, basting frequently with the remaining marinade, for about 15 minutes until the chicken is cooked. Serve with the red bell pepper sauce.

5

ginger chicken & corn

Chicken wings and corn in a sticky ginger marinade are designed to be eaten with the fingers—there's no other way!

Serves 6

3 fresh corn cobs

12 chicken wings

1 inch piece fresh gingerroot

6 tbsp lemon juice

4 tsp sunflower oil

1 tbsp superfine sugar

cook's tip

Cut off the wing tips before broiling as they burn very easily. Alternatively, you can cover them with small pieces of foil.

cook's tip

When you are buying fresh corn, look for plump, tightly packed kernels. If fresh corn is unavailable, you can use thawed frozen corn instead.

1

2

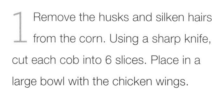

4

1 Remove the husks and silken hairs from the corn. Using a sharp knife, cut each cob into 6 slices. Place in a large bowl with the chicken wings.

2 Peel and grate the gingerroot or chop finely.

3 Mix the gingerroot with the lemon juice, sunflower oil, and superfine sugar, then toss with the corn and chicken to coat.

4 Thread the corn and chicken wings on to skewers, to make turning easier.

5 Cook the corn and chicken under a preheated moderately hot broiler or grill for 15–20 minutes, basting with the gingery glaze and turning frequently until the corn is golden brown and tender, and the chicken is cooked. Serve with jacket potatoes or salad.

sesame brochettes with cranberry sauce

The cranberries give the sauce a lovely tart flavor. These little kabobs are delicious and can be served hot or cold.

Serves 8

4 chicken breasts, skinned and boned

4 tbsp dry white wine

1 tbsp light brown sugar

2 tbsp sunflower oil

salt and pepper

3½ oz sesame seeds

green salad leaves and boiled new potatoes,
    to serve

SAUCE

6 oz cranberries

⅔ cup cranberry juice drink

2 tbsp light brown sugar

2

3

5

1 Cut the chicken into 1 inch pieces. Put the wine, sugar, oil, and salt and pepper to taste in a large bowl, stirring to combine. Add the chicken pieces and toss to coat. Leave to marinate for at least 30 minutes, turning the chicken occasionally.

2 To make the sauce, place the ingredients in a small pan and bring slowly to a boil, stirring. Simmer gently for 5–10 minutes until the cranberries are soft and pulpy. Taste and add a little extra sugar if wished. Keep warm or leave to chill as required.

3 Remove the chicken pieces from the marinade with a draining spoon. Thread the chicken pieces on to 8 skewers, spacing them slightly apart to ensure even cooking.

4 Grill on an oiled rack over hot coals for 4–5 minutes on each side until just cooked. Brush several times with the marinade during cooking.

5 Remove the chicken skewers from the rack and roll in the sesame seeds. Return to the grill and cook for about 1 minute on each side or until the sesame seeds are toasted. Serve with the cranberry sauce, new potatoes, and green salad leaves.

variation

Cranberry sauce goes well with all types of poultry. Try it with turkey or guinea fowl.

chicken kabobs

These kabobs are a deliciously different way of serving chicken. Serve with dhal and chapatis for a real indian feel.

1

Serves 6-8

3 lb 5 oz chicken, boned

½ tsp ground cumin

4 cardamom seeds, ground

½ tsp ground cinnamon

1 tsp salt

1 tsp fresh ginger root, finely chopped

1 tsp fresh garlic, finely chopped

½ tsp ground allspice

½ tsp pepper

1¼ cups water

2 tbsp yogurt

2 green chiles

1 small onion

fresh cilantro leaves

1 medium egg, beaten

1¼ cups oil

salad greens and lemon wedges, to garnish

2

cook's tip

Indian kabob dishes are not necessarily cooked on a skewer; they can also be served in a dish and are always dry dishes with no sauce.

1 Place the boned chicken in a large pan. Add the ground cumin, cardamom seeds, ground cinnamon, salt, gingerroot, garlic, ground allspice, and pepper and pour in the water. Bring the mixture to a boil until all of the water has been absorbed.

2 Put the mixture in a food processor and grind to form a smooth paste. Transfer the paste to a mixing bowl. Add the yogurt and blend together until well combined.

3 Place the green chiles, onion, and cilantro leaves in the food processor and grind finely. Add to the chicken mixture and mix well. Add the beaten egg and mix to combine.

4 Break off 12–15 portions from the mixture and make small, flat round shapes in the palm of your hand.

5 Heat the oil in a pan and sauté the kabobs gently, in batches, over a low heat, turning once. Drain thoroughly on kitchen paper and serve hot.

3

thai-style chicken skewers

Here the chicken is marinated in a delicious aromatic sauce before being threaded on to skewers.

Serves 4

4 chicken breasts, skinned and boned

1 onion, peeled and cut into wedges

1 large red bell pepper, seeded

1 large yellow bell pepper, seeded

12 kaffir lime leaves

2 tbsp sunflower oil

2 tbsp lime juice

tomato halves, to serve

MARINADE

1 tbsp Thai red curry paste

⅔ cup canned coconut milk

cook's tip

Cooking the marinade first intensifies the flavor. It is important to allow the marinade to cool before adding the chicken, or bacteria may breed in the warm temperature. You will find fresh kaffir lime leaves in Asian stores, but if these are unavailable, bay leaves can be used instead.

1 To make the marinade, place the red curry paste in a small pan over medium heat and cook for 1 minute. Add half of the coconut milk to the pan and bring the mixture to a boil. Boil for 2–3 minutes until the liquid has reduced by about two-thirds.

2 Remove the pan from the heat and stir in the remaining coconut milk. Set aside to cool.

3 Cut the chicken into 1 inch pieces. Stir the chicken into the cold marinade, cover, and leave to chill for at least 2 hours.

4 Cut the onion into wedges and the bell peppers into 1 inch pieces.

1

3

5 Remove the chicken pieces from the marinade and thread them on to skewers, alternating the chicken with the vegetables and lime leaves.

6 Combine the oil and lime juice in a small bowl and brush the mixture over the kabobs. Grill the skewers over hot coals, turning and basting frequently for 10–15 minutes until the chicken is cooked through. Grill the tomato halves and serve with the chicken skewers.

minty lime chicken

These tangy lime and honey-coated pieces have a matching sauce or dip based on creamy unsweetened yogurt. They could be served at a barbecue or as a main course for a dinner party.

Serves 6

3 tbsp finely chopped mint

4 tbsp clear honey

4 tbsp lime juice

12 boneless chicken thighs

SAUCE

½ cup thick unsweetened yogurt

1 tbsp finely chopped mint

2 tsp finely grated lime peel

salad, to serve

variation

Use this marinade for chicken kabobs, alternating the chicken with lime and red onion wedges.

cooks tip

Mint can be grown very easily in a garden or window box. It is a useful herb for marinades and salad dressings. Other useful herbs to grow are parsley and basil.

1

2

1 Combine the mint, honey, and lime juice in a bowl.

2 Use toothpicks to keep the chicken thighs in neat shapes and add the chicken to the marinade, turning to coat evenly.

3 Leave to marinate for at least 30 minutes, preferably overnight. Cook the chicken on a preheated moderate broiler or over hot coals, turning frequently and basting with the marinade. The chicken is cooked if the juices run clear when the chicken is pierced in the thickest part with a skewer.

4

4 Meanwhile, mix together the sauce ingredients.

5 Remove the toothpicks and serve the chicken with a salad and the sauce.

indian charred chicken

This delicious dish has an Indian-influenced flavor. Serve with naan bread and a cucumber raita to complete the effect.

Serves 4

4 chicken breasts, skinned and boned

2 tbsp curry paste

1 tbsp sunflower oil

1 tbsp light muscovado sugar

1 tsp ground ginger

½ tsp ground cumin

naan bread and green salad leaves, to serve

CUCUMBER RAITA

¼ cucumber

salt

⅔ cup unsweetened yogurt

¼ tsp chili powder

cook's tip

Flattening the chicken breasts makes them thinner so that they cook more quickly.

1

2

3

1 Place the chicken breasts between 2 sheets of baking parchment or plastic wrap. Pound them with the flat side of a meat mallet or rolling pin to flatten them.

2 Mix together the curry paste, oil, sugar, ginger, and cumin in a small bowl. Spread the mixture over both sides of the chicken and set aside until required.

3 To make the raita, peel the cucumber and scoop out the seeds with a spoon. Grate the cucumber flesh, sprinkle with salt, place in a strainer, and leave to stand for 10 minutes. Rinse off the salt and squeeze out any moisture by pressing the cucumber with the base of a glass or back of a spoon.

4 Mix the cucumber with the yogurt and stir in the chili powder. Leave to chill until required.

5 Transfer the chicken to a rack and grill for 10 minutes.

6 Warm the naan bread at the side of the barbecue. Serve the chicken with the naan bread and raita and accompanied with fresh green salad leaves.

chicken quarters with warm mayonnaise

Chicken quarters are grilled, then served with a strongly flavored garlic mayonnaise, which originated in Provence, France.

Serves 4

4 chicken quarters

2 tbsp oil

2 tbsp lemon juice

2 tsp dried thyme

salt and pepper

green salad and lemon slices, to serve

AIOLI

5 garlic cloves, finely chopped

2 egg yolks

½ cup each olive oil and sunflower oil

1 tsp lemon juice

1 tbsp boiling water

1 Using a skewer, prick the chicken quarters in several places and place them in a shallow dish.

2 Combine the oil, lemon juice, thyme, and seasoning, then pour over the chicken, turning to coat the chicken evenly. Set aside for 2 hours.

3 To make the aioli, beat together the garlic and a pinch of salt to make a paste. Add the egg yolks and beat well. Gradually add the oils, drop by drop, beating vigorously, until the mayonnaise

becomes creamy and smooth. Add the oils in a thin steady trickle and continue beating until the aioli is thick. Stir in the lemon juice and season with pepper. Set aside in a warm place.

4 Place the chicken over preheated coals and cook for 25–30 minutes. Brush with the marinade and turn the portions to cook evenly. Remove and arrange on a serving plate.

5 Beat the water into the aioli and turn into a warmed serving bowl. Serve the chicken with the aioli, a green salad, and lemon slices.

cook's tip

To make a quick aioli, add the garlic to 1¼ cups good quality mayonnaise then place in a bowl over a pan of warm water and beat together. Just before serving add 1–2 tbsp hot water.

favorite grilled chicken

These chicken wings are brushed with a simple grill glaze, which can be made in minutes, but the results are sure to delight everyone.

Serves 4

8 chicken wings or 1 chicken cut into
   8 portions

3 tbsp tomato paste

3 tbsp brown fruity sauce

1 tbsp white wine vinegar

1 tbsp honey

1 tbsp olive oil

1 clove garlic, crushed (optional)

salad greens, to serve

variation

This grill glaze also makes a very good baste to brush over pork chops.

cook's tip

When poultry is cooked over a very hot grill, the heat immediately seals in all of the juices, leaving the meat succulent. For this reason make sure that the coals are hot enough before starting to grill.

1 Remove the skin from the chicken if you want to reduce the fat in the dish.

2 To make the barbecue glaze, place the tomato paste, brown fruity sauce, white wine vinegar, honey, oil, and garlic in a small bowl. Stir all of the ingredients together until they are thoroughly blended.

3 Brush the grill glaze over the chicken and grill over hot coals for 15–20 minutes. Turn the chicken portions over occasionally and baste frequently with the grill glaze. If the chicken begins to blacken before it is cooked, raise the rack if possible or move the chicken to a cooler part of the grill to slow down the cooking.

4 Transfer the grilled chicken to warm serving plates and serve with fresh salad leaves.

2

3

1

sweet maple chicken

You can use any chicken portions for this recipe. Boned chicken thighs are economical for large barbecue parties, but you could also use wings or drumsticks.

Serves 6

2 boned chicken thighs

5 tbsp maple syrup

1 tbsp superfine sugar

grated peel and juice of ½ orange

2 tbsp tomato catsup

2 tsp Worcestershire sauce

slices of orange and sprig of flat-leaf parsley,
   to garnish

focaccia bread, salad leaves, and cherry
   tomatoes, quartered, to serve

1

3

1 Using a sharp knife, make 2–3 slashes in the flesh of the chicken. Place the chicken in a shallow, nonmetallic dish.

2 To make the marinade, mix together the maple syrup, sugar, orange peel, and juice, catsup, and Worcestershire sauce in a small bowl.

3 Pour the marinade over the chicken, tossing the chicken to coat thoroughly. Cover and leave to chill in the refrigerator until required.

4 Remove the chicken from the marinade, reserving the marinade for basting.

5 Transfer the chicken to the grill and cook over hot coals for 20 minutes, turning the chicken and basting with the marinade frequently.

6 Transfer the chicken to serving plates and garnish with slices of orange and a sprig of fresh-leaf parsley. Serve with focaccia bread, fresh salad leaves, and cherry tomatoes.

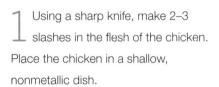

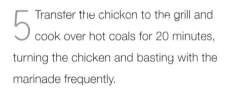

5

cook's tip

If time is short you can omit the marinating time. If you use chicken quarters, rather than the smaller thigh portions, par-boil them for 10 minutes before brushing with the marinade and grilling.

chicken cajun-style

These spicy chicken wings are good served with a chili salsa and salad.
Alternatively, if this is too spicy for your taste, try a sour cream and chive dip.

Serves 4

16 chicken wings

4 tsp paprika

2 tsp ground coriander

1 tsp celery salt

1 tsp ground cumin

½ tsp cayenne pepper

½ tsp salt

1 tbsp oil

2 tbsp red wine vinegar

fresh parsley, to garnish

cherry tomatoes and mixed salad greens,
   to serve

1

3

2

3 Rub this mixture over the wings to coat evenly and set aside, in the refrigerator, for at least 1 hour to allow the flavors to permeate the chicken.

4 Cook the chicken wings on a preheated grill, occasionally brushing with oil, for about 15 minutes, turning often until cooked through. Garnish with fresh parsley and serve with cherry tomatoes, mixed salad greens, and a sauce of your choice.

1 Wash the chicken wings and pat dry with paper towels. Remove the wing tips with kitchen scissors.

2 Mix together the paprika, coriander, celery salt, cumin, cayenne pepper, salt, oil, and red wine vinegar.

variation

Although chicken wings do not have much meat on them, they are small and easy to pick up with your fingers which makes them ideal for barbecues. However, they can also be enjoyed fried or roasted.

cook's tip

To save time, you can buy ready-made Cajun spice seasoning to rub over the chicken wings.

broiled chicken & vegetable salad

Broiling is a quick, healthy cooking method, ideal for sealing in the juices and flavor of chicken breasts, and a wonderful way to cook summer vegetables.

Serves 4

1 small eggplant, sliced

salt

2 garlic cloves, crushed

finely grated rind of ½ lemon

1 tbsp chopped fresh mint

6 tbsp olive oil

pepper

4 boneless chicken breasts

2 medium zucchini, sliced

1 medium red bell pepper, quartered

1 small bulb fennel, sliced thickly

1 large red onion, sliced thickly

1 small ciabatta loaf or 1 French baguette,
    sliced

extra olive oil

1

3

4

4 Combine the eggplant and the
remaining vegetables, then toss
in the remaining oil mixture. Marinate
the chicken and vegetables for about
30 minutes.

5 Place the chicken breasts and
vegetables on a preheated hot
broiler or grill, and turning occasionally,
until they are golden brown and tender,
or cook on a ridged griddle pan on
the hob.

6 Brush the bread slices with olive oil
and broil until golden.

7 Drizzle a little olive oil over the
chicken and grilled vegetables and
serve hot or cold with the crusty bread
toasts.

1 Place the eggplant slices in a
colander and sprinkle with salt.
Leave over a bowl to drain for 30
minutes, rinse, and dry. This will get rid
of the bitter juices.

2 Mix together the garlic, lemon peel,
mint, and olive oil, and season.

3 Slash the chicken breasts at
intervals with a sharp knife. Spoon
over about half of the oil mixture and stir
to combine all the ingredients.

spicy sesame chicken

This is a quick and easy recipe for the grill, perfect for lunch or to eat outdoors on a picnic because it is easy to transport.

Serves 4

4 chicken quarters

½ cup unsweetened yogurt

finely grated peel and juice of 1 small lemon

2 tsp medium-hot curry paste

1 tbsp sesame seeds

salad, naan bread and lemon wedges,
    to serve

1

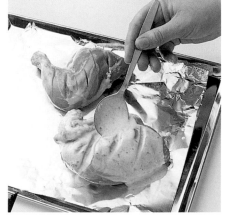

3

2

1 Remove the skin from the chicken and make cuts in the flesh at intervals with a sharp knife.

2 Combine the unsweetened yogurt, lemon peel, lemon juice, and curry paste in a bowl to form a smooth mixture.

3 Spoon the mixture over the chicken and arrange on a foil-lined broiler pan or cookie sheet.

variation

Poppy seeds, fennel seeds,
or cumin seeds, or a mixture
of all three, can also be used
to sprinkle over the chicken.

cook's tip

If you have time, leave the
chicken and the sauce in the
refrigerator to marinate
overnight so the flavors are
fully absorbed.

4 Place the chicken quarters under a preheated moderately hot broiler and broil for 12–15 minutes, turning once. Broil until golden brown and thoroughly cooked. Just before the end of the cooking time, sprinkle the chicken with the sesame seeds.

5 Serve with a salad, naan bread, and lemon wedges.

sweet & sour drumsticks

Chicken drumsticks are marinated to impart a tangy sweet and sour flavor and a shiny glaze. Make sure they are cooked through thoroughly.

Serves 4

8 chicken drumsticks

4 tbsp red wine vinegar

2 tbsp tomato paste

2 tbsp soy sauce

2 tbsp honey

1 tbsp Worcestershire sauce

1 garlic clove

good pinch cayenne pepper

sprig of fresh parsley, to garnish

crisp salad, to serve

cook's tip

For a tangy flavor, add the juice of 1 lime to the marinade. While the drumsticks are grilling, check regularly to ensure that they are not burning.

variation

This sweet and sour marinade would also work well with pork or shrimp. Thread pork cubes or shrimp on to skewers with bell peppers and button onions.

1

2

3

1 Skin the chicken, if desired, and slash 2–3 times with a sharp knife.

2 Lay the chicken drumsticks side by side in a shallow non-metallic container.

3 Mix the red wine vinegar, tomato paste, soy sauce, honey, Worcestershire sauce, garlic, and cayenne pepper together and pour over the chicken drumsticks.

4 Leave to marinate in the refrigerator for 1 hour. Cook the drumsticks on a preheated grill for about 20 minutes, brushing with the marinade and turning during cooking. Garnish with parsley and serve with a crisp salad.

chicken with garden herbs

Warm weather calls for lighter eating, and this chilled chicken dish in a subtle herb vinaigrette is ideal for a summer dinner party, or for a picnic.

Serves 4

4 part-boned, skinless chicken breasts

6 tbsp olive oil

2 tbsp lemon juice

4 tbsp finely chopped summer herbs,
    such as parsley, chives and mint

pepper

1 ripe avocado

½ cup low-fat fromage blanc

cold rice, to serve

1

4

5

1 Using a sharp knife, cut 3–4 deep
slashes in the chicken breasts.

2 Place in a flameproof dish and
brush lightly with a little of the oil.

3 Cook the chicken on a preheated
moderately hot broiler turning once
until golden and the juices run clear
when the chicken is pierced in the
thickest part with a skewer.

4 Combine the remaining oil with the
lemon juice and herbs and season
with pepper. Spoon the oil over the
chicken and leave to cool. Chill in the
refrigerator for at least 1 hour.

5 Mash the avocado or purée in a
food processor with the fromage
blanc. Season with pepper to taste.
Serve the chicken with the avocado
sauce and rice.

cook's tip

The chicken can be cooked
several hours before you need
it and stored in the
refrigerator until required.

cook's tip

To remove the stone easily
from an avocado, first cut the
avocado in half. Holding one
half securely in your hand,
rap the knife into the stone
so that it becomes embedded in
the stone, then carefully
twist the knife to dislodge
the stone.

jerk chicken

This is perhaps one of the best known Caribbean dishes. The "jerk" in the name refers to the hot spicy coating.

Serves 4

4 chicken portions

1 bunch scallions, trimmed

1–2 Scotch Bonnet chiles, seeded

1 garlic clove

2 inch piece ginger root, peeled and
  roughly chopped

½ tsp dried thyme

½ tsp paprika

¼ tsp ground allspice

pinch ground cinnamon

pinch ground cloves

4 tbsp white wine vinegar

3 tbsp light soy sauce

pepper

cook's tip

As Jamaican cuisine becomes increasingly popular, you will find jars of ready-made jerk marinade, which you can use when time is short. Allow the chicken to marinate for as long as possible for maximum flavor.

variation

You can use milder chiles or alternatively increase the amount of chile used.

2

3

4

1 Rinse the chicken portions and pat them dry on paper towels. Place them in a shallow dish.

2 Place the scallions, chiles, garlic, ginger root, thyme, paprika, allspice, cinnamon, cloves, wine vinegar, soy sauce, and pepper to taste in a food processor and process to make a smooth mixture.

3 Pour the spicy mixture over the chicken. Turn the chicken portions over so that they are well coated in the marinade. Transfer the chicken to the refrigerator and leave to marinate for up to 24 hours.

4 Remove the chicken from the marinade and grill over medium hot coals for about 30 minutes, turning the chicken over and basting occasionally with any remaining marinade, until the chicken is cooked through.

5 Transfer the chicken portions to individual serving plates and serve at once.

sticky chicken drumsticks

These drumsticks are always popular with children—make sure there are plenty of napkins for wiping sticky fingers or provide finger bowls with a slice of lemon.

Serves 10

10 chicken drumsticks

4 tbsp fine-cut orange marmalade

1 tbsp Worcestershire sauce

grated peel and juice of ½ orange

salt and pepper

cherry tomatoes and salad leaves, to serve

cook's tip

Par-cooking the chicken is an ideal way of making sure that it is cooked through without becoming overcooked and burned on the outside.

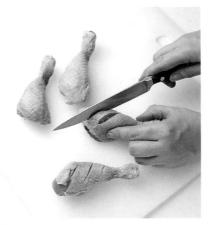

1

1 Using a sharp knife, make 2–3 slashes in the flesh of each chicken drumstick.

2 Bring a large saucepan of water to a boil and add the chicken drumsticks. Cover the pan, return to a boil, and cook for 5–10 minutes. Remove the chicken and drain thoroughly.

3 Meanwhile, make the baste. Place the orange marmalade, Worcestershire sauce, orange peel and juice, and salt and pepper to taste in a small saucepan. Heat gently, stirring continuously, until the marmalade melts and all of the ingredients are well combined.

4 Brush the baste over the par-cooked chicken drumsticks and transfer them to the grill to complete cooking. Grill over hot coals for about 10 minutes, turning and basting frequently with the remaining baste.

2

3

5 Carefully thread 3 cherry tomatoes on to a skewer and transfer to the barbecue for 1–2 minutes.

6 Transfer the chicken drumsticks to serving plates. Serve with the cherry tomato skewers and a selection of fresh salad leaves.

chicken skewers with lemon & cilantro

A tangy lemon yogurt is served with this tasty chicken dish.

Serves 4

4 chicken breasts, skinned and boned

1 tsp ground coriander

2 tsp lemon juice

1 lemon

salt and pepper

1¼ cups unsweetened yogurt

2 tbsp chopped, fresh cilantro

oil for brushing

1 Cut the chicken into 1 inch pieces and place them in a shallow, non–metallic dish.

2 Add the coriander, lemon juice, salt and pepper to taste, and 4 tbsp of the yogurt to the chicken and mix together until thoroughly combined. Cover and leave to chill for at least 2 hours, preferably overnight.

3

3 To make the lemon yogurt, peel and finely chop the lemon, discarding any pips. Stir the lemon into the yogurt together with the fresh cilantro. Leave to chill in the refrigerator until required.

4 Thread the chicken pieces on to skewers. Brush the rack with oil and grill the chicken over hot coals for about 15 minutes, basting with the oil.

5 Transfer the chicken kabobs to warm serving plates and garnish with a sprig of fresh cilantro, lemon wedges, and fresh salad leaves. Serve with the lemon yogurt.

1

cooks tip

These kabobs are delicious served on a bed of blanched spinach, which has been seasoned with salt, pepper, and nutmeg.

variation

Prepare the chicken the day before it is needed so that it can marinate overnight. This will allow the flavors to be fully absorbed.

2

skewered chicken with bramble sauce

This fall recipe can be made with fresh-picked wild blackberries from the hedgerow if you're lucky enough to have a good supply.

Serves 4

4 chicken breasts or 8 thighs

4 tbsp dry white wine or cider

2 tbsp chopped fresh rosemary

pepper

rosemary sprigs

  and blackberries, to garnish

green salad, to serve

SAUCE

scant 2 cups blackberries

1 tbsp cider vinegar

2 tbsp redcurrant jelly

¼ tsp grated nutmeg

1

2

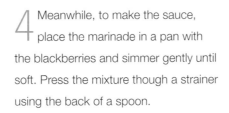

5

1 Using a sharp knife, cut the chicken into 1 inch pieces and place in a bowl. Sprinkle over the white wine and rosemary, and season well with pepper. Cover and leave to marinate for at least an hour.

2 Drain the chicken, reserving the marinade, and thread the meat on to 8 skewers.

3 Cook on a preheated moderately hot broiler for 8–10 minutes, turning, until golden and evenly cooked.

4 Meanwhile, to make the sauce, place the marinade in a pan with the blackberries and simmer gently until soft. Press the mixture though a strainer using the back of a spoon.

5 Return the blackberry purée to the pan with the cider vinegar and redcurrant jelly and bring to a boil. Boil uncovered until the sauce is reduced by about one-third.

6 Spoon a little bramble sauce on to each plate and place a chicken skewer on top. Sprinkle with nutmeg and serve hot. Garnish with rosemary and blackberries and serve with a green salad.

cook's tip

If you use canned fruit, omit the redcurrant jelly.

skewered chicken spirals

These unusual chicken kabobs have a wonderful Mediterranean flavor, and the bacon helps keep them moist during cooking.

4

Serves 4

4 skinless, boneless chicken breasts

1 garlic clove, finely chopped

2 tbsp tomato paste

4 slices smoked back bacon

large handful fresh basil leaves

salt and pepper

oil for brushing

green salad, to serve

1 Spread out a piece of chicken between two sheets of plastic wrap and beat firmly with a rolling pin to flatten the chicken to an even thickness. Repeat with the remaining pieces of chicken.

2 Mix together the garlic and tomato paste until well blended. Spread the mixture evenly over the chicken.

3 Lay a bacon slice over each piece of chicken, then scatter with the fresh basil leaves. Season well with salt and pepper.

4 Roll up each piece of chicken firmly, then cut into thick slices using a sharp knife.

5 Thread the slices securely on to four skewers, making sure the skewer holds the chicken in a spiral shape.

6 Brush the skewers lightly with oil and cook on preheated hot coals or grill for about 5 minutes, turn the skewers over, and cook for a further 5 minutes, until the chicken is cooked through. Serve the chicken spirals hot with a green salad.

1

3

cook's tip

Flattening the chicken breasts makes them thinner so that they cook more quickly. It also makes them easier to roll.

cook's tip

To complete the Mediterranean theme, serve these kabobs with Parmesan-topped garlic bread.

marinated chicken with satay sauce

This is an ideal sauce to accompany food cooked on the grill, and it can be kept warm at the side of the rack.

Serves 4

2 chicken breasts, skinned and boned

MARINADE

4 tbsp sunflower oil

2 cloves garlic, finely chopped

3 tbsp fresh, chopped cilantro

1 tbsp superfine sugar

½ tsp ground cumin

½ tsp ground coriander

1 tbsp soy sauce

1 red or green chile, seeded

salt and pepper

SAUCE

2 tbsp sunflower oil

1 small onion, chopped finely

1 red or green chile, seeded and chopped

½ tsp ground coriander

½ tsp ground cumin

8 tbsp peanut butter

8 tbsp chicken bouillon or water

1 tbsp block coconut

1 Soak 8 wooden skewers in large, shallow dish of cold water for at least 30 minutes. This process will prevent the skewers from burning during grilling.

1

2 Cut the chicken lengthwise into 8 long strips. Thread the strips of chicken, concertina-style, on to the skewers and set aside while you make the marinade.

3 Place the ingredients for the marinade in a food processor and process until smooth.

2

4 Coat the chicken with the marinade paste, cover, and leave to chill in the refrigerator for at least 2 hours.

5 To make the sauce, heat the oil in a small pan and sauté the onion and chile until they are softened but not browned. Stir in the spices and cook for 1 minute. Add the remaining sauce ingredients and cook the mixture gently for 5 minutes. Keep warm at the side of the grill.

6 Grill the chicken skewers over hot coals for about 10 minutes, basting with any remaining marinade. Serve with the warm sauce.

5

mustardy barbecue drummers

Great for grills, or for simple summer lunches and picnics, this is an easy and tasty recipe for chicken drumsticks.

Serves 4

10 slices smoked streaky bacon

1 garlic clove, peeled and finely chopped

3 tbsp whole grain mustard

4 tbsp fresh brown bread crumbs

8 chicken drumsticks

1 tbsp sunflower oil

fresh parsley sprigs, to garnish

cook's tip

Don't cook the chicken over the hottest part of the barbecue or the outside may be charred before the center is cooked.

1

1 Chop two of the bacon slices into small pieces and dry fry for 3–4 minutes, stirring so that the bacon does not stick to the bottom of the pan. Remove from the heat and stir in the garlic, 2 tablespoons of wholegrain mustard, and the bread crumbs.

2

2 Carefully loosen the skin from each drumstick with your fingers, being careful not to tear the skin. Spoon a little of the mustard stuffing under each flap of skin, smoothing the skins over firmly afterward.

3 Wrap a bacon rasher around each drumstick, and secure with toothpicks.

3

4 Mix together the remaining mustard and the oil, brush over the chicken drumsticks, and cook on a preheated moderately hot barbecue or broiler for about 25 minutes, until there is no trace of pink in the juices when the thickest part of the chicken is pierced with a skewer.

5 Garnish with the parsley sprigs and serve hot or cold.

tropical chicken skewers

In this recipe, chicken is given a Caribbean flavor. The marinade keeps it moist and succulent during cooking.

Serves 6

1 lb 10 oz boneless
   chicken breasts

2 tbsp medium sherry

pepper

3 mangoes

bay leaves

2 tbsp oil

2 tbsp coarsely shredded coconut

crisp salad, to serve

1 Remove the skin from the chicken and cut into 1 inch cubes and toss in the sherry, with a little pepper.

2 Using a sharp knife, cut the mangoes into 1 inch cubes, discarding the stone and skin.

3 Thread the chicken, mango cubes, and bay leaves alternately on to long skewers, then brush lightly with oil.

1

2

4 Broil the skewers on a preheated moderately hot broiler for about 8–10 minutes, turning occasionally until golden.

5 Sprinkle the skewers with the coconut and broil for a further 30 seconds. Serve with a crisp salad.

3

cook's tip

Use mangoes that are ripe but still firm so that they hold together on the skewers during cooking. Another firm fruit that would be suitable is pineapple.

cook's tip

Remember that if you are using metal skewers, they will get very hot, so be sure to use gloves or tongs to turn them. Wooden skewers should be soaked in water for 30 minutes before use to prevent them from burning on the barbecue, and the exposed ends should be covered with pieces of kitchen foil.

skewered spicy tomato chicken

These low-fat, spicy skewers are cooked in a matter of minutes—and they can be assembled ahead of time and stored in the refrigerator until you need them.

Serves 4

1 lb 2 oz skinless, boneless chicken breasts

3 tbsp tomato paste

2 tbsp honey

2 tbsp Worcestershire sauce

1 tbsp chopped fresh rosemary

9 oz cherry tomatoes

couscous or rice, to serve

sprigs of rosemary, to garnish

1

1 Using a sharp knife, cut the chicken into 1 inch chunks and place in a bowl.

2 Mix together the tomato paste, honey, Worcestershire sauce, and rosemary. Add to the chicken, stirring to coat evenly.

3 Alternating the chicken pieces and tomatoes, thread them on to eight wooden skewers.

2

4 Spoon over any remaining glaze. Cook under a preheated hot broiler for 8–10 minutes, turning occasionally, until the chicken is thoroughly cooked. Serve on a bed of couscous or rice and garnish with sprigs of rosemary.

cook's tip

Couscous is made from semolina that has been made into separate grains. It is very easy to prepare—simply soak it in a bowl of boiling water and then fluff up the grains with a fork. Flavorings such as lemon or nutmeg can be added.

cook's tip

Cherry tomatoes are ideal for barbecues as they can be threaded straight on to skewers. As they are kept whole, the skins keep in the tomatoes' natural juices.

broiled chicken with pesto toasts

This Italian-style dish is richly flavored with pesto, which is a mixture of basil, olive oil, pine nuts, and Parmesan cheese. Either red or green pesto can be used for this recipe.

Serves 4

8 part-boned chicken thighs

olive oil, for brushing

1⅔ cups sieved tomatoes

½ cup green or red pesto sauce

12 slices French bread

1 cup freshly grated Parmesan cheese

½ cup pine nuts or slivered almonds

salad leaves, to serve

1

2

1 Arrange the chicken in a single layer in a wide flameproof dish and brush lightly with oil. Place under a preheated broiler for about 15 minutes, turning occasionally, until golden brown.

2 Pierce the chicken with a skewer to ensure that there is no trace of pink in the juices.

3 Pour off any excess fat. Warm the sieved tomatoes and half the pesto sauce in a small pan and pour over the chicken. Broil for a few more minutes, turning until coated.

4 Meanwhile, spread the remaining pesto on to the slices of bread. Arrange the bread over the chicken and sprinkle with the Parmesan cheese. Scatter the pine nuts over the cheese. Broil for 2–3 minutes, or until browned and bubbling. Serve with a selection of salad leaves.

4

cook's tip

Although leaving the skin on the chicken means that it will have a higher fat content, many people like the rich taste and crispy skin, especially when it is blackened by the grill. The skin also keeps in the cooking juices.

broiled poussin with lemon & tarragon

Spatchcocked baby chickens are complemented by the delicate
fragrance of lemon and tarragon and broiled.

Serves 2

2 baby chickens

4 sprigs fresh tarragon

1 tsp oil

2 tbsp butter

rind of ½ lemon

1 tbsp lemon juice

1 garlic clove, crushed

salt and pepper

tarragon and orange slices, to garnish

1 Prepare the baby chickens, turn
them breast-side down on a
chopping board and cut them through
the backbone using kitchen scissors.
Crush each bird gently to break the
bones so that they lie flat while cooking.
Season each with salt.

2 Turn them over and insert a sprig of
tarragon under the skin over each
side of the breast.

3 Brush the chickens with oil, using
a pastry brush, and place under a
preheated hot broiler about 5 inches
from the heat. Broil the chickens for
about 15 minutes, turning half way, until
they are lightly browned.

4 Meanwhile, to make the glaze, melt
the butter in a small saucepan, add
the lemon rind, lemon juice and garlic
and season with salt and pepper.

5 Brush the baby chickens with the
glaze and cook for a further 15
minutes, turning them once and
brushing regularly so that they stay
moist. Garnish the chickens with
tarragon and orange slices and serve
with new potatoes.

2

4

1

cook's tip

Once the chickens are
flattened, insert 2 metal
skewers through them to keep
them flat.

spatchcock baby chicken with garlic & herbs

It is not difficult to spatchcock (open out) baby chickens, and it is the best way to cook whole birds on the grill.

Serves 2

2 baby chickens, 1lb

¾ oz butter

2 cloves garlic, crushed

2 tbsp chopped, mixed fresh herbs

BASTE

4 tbsp olive oil

2 tbsp lemon juice

2 tbsp chopped, mixed herbs

salt and pepper

cook's tip

Use a combination of whatever fresh herbs you have to hand. Thyme, rosemary, mint, oregano, parsley, or cilantro are all suitable. If you want to cook a whole chicken in this way double the amount of baste and cook for 40–50 minutes.

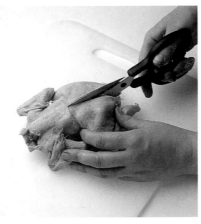

1

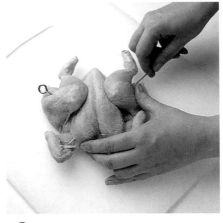

3

1

1 To spatchcock each chicken, place each bird on its breast and use sharp scissors or poultry shears to cut along the length of the back bone. Open out the bird as much as possible and place it breast-side up on a chopping board. Press down firmly on the breast bone to break it.

2 Mix together the butter, garlic and herbs until well combined. Lift up the skin from the breast of each chicken. Divide the butter equally between the 2 chickens and spread over the breast under the skin.

3 Open out each bird. Thread 2 skewers diagonally through each bird to hold it flat.

4 Mix together the ingredients for the baste in a bowl.

5 Place the birds, bone-side down, over medium hot coals and grill for 25 minutes, basting with the lemon and herb baste. Turn the birds over and grill, skin-side down, for 15 minutes, basting frequently, or until cooked through.

Because chicken is popular throughout the world, there are countless spicy recipes from Asia, Mexico, the Caribbean, Spain, and Japan. Lime juice, peanut, coconut and chili add the authentic tastes of Thailand to Chili Coconut Chicken, while Kashmiri Chicken is a rich and spicy dish from Northern India with an aromatic sauce made from yogurt, Tikka curry paste, cumin, ginger, chile, and almonds. From Spain comes Spanish Chicken with Shrimp with its unusual mixture of chicken and shellfish, together with the famous spicy Spanish sausage, chorizo, slow-cooked in a sauce of garlic, tomatoes, and white wine. Cumin-Spiced Apricot Chicken is a creative modern dish that would be perfect for any special occasion. The chicken is stuffed with dried apricots, coated in a yogurt, cumin, and turmeric sauce and served with

nutty rice. There is even a dish from Japan, Teppanyaki, a simple dish of sautéd chicken slices with bell peppers, scallions, and beansprouts, served with a mirin dipping sauce.

dishes for
entertaining

chicken, carrot & noodle stir-fry

The chicken and noodles are cooked and then a flavored egg mixture is tossed into the dish to coat the noodles and meat in this delicious recipe.

Serves 4

9 oz egg noodles

1 lb chicken thighs

2 tbsp groundnut oil

3½ oz carrots, sliced

3 tbsp oyster sauce

2 eggs

3 tbsp cold water

variation

Flavor the eggs with soy sauce or hoisin sauce as an alternative to the oyster sauce, if you prefer.

1 Place the egg noodles in a large bowl or dish. Pour enough boiling water over the noodles to cover and leave to stand for 10 minutes.

2 Meanwhile, remove the skin from the chicken thighs. Cut the chicken flesh into small pieces, using a sharp knife.

3 Heat the groundnut oil in a large preheated wok.

4 Add the pieces of chicken and the carrot slices to the wok and stir-fry the mixture for about 5 minutes.

5 Drain the noodles thoroughly. Add the noodles to the wok and stir-fry for a further 2–3 minutes or until the noodles are heated through.

2

4

6 Beat together the oyster sauce, eggs and 3 tablespoons of cold water. Drizzle the mixture over the noodles and stir-fry for a further 2–3 minutes or until the eggs set. Transfer to warm serving bowls and serve hot.

1

chicken, pepper & mushroom stir-fry

Ready-made yellow bean sauce is available from large stores and Chinese food stores. It is made from yellow soya beans and is quite salty in flavor.

Serves 4

1 lb skinless, boneless chicken breasts

1 egg white, beaten

1 tbsp cornstarch

1 tbsp rice wine vinegar

1 tbsp light soy sauce

1 tsp superfine sugar

3 tbsp vegetable oil

1 garlic clove, crushed

½-inch piece fresh ginger root, grated

1 green bell pepper, seeded and diced

2 large mushrooms, sliced

3 tbsp yellow bean sauce

yellow or green bell pepper strips, to garnish

variation

Black bean sauce would work equally well with this recipe. Although this would affect the appearance of the dish, as it is much darker in color, the flavors would be compatible.

1 Trim any fat from the chicken and cut the meat into 1 inch cubes.

2 Mix the egg white and cornstarch in a shallow bowl. Add the chicken and turn in the mixture to coat. Set aside for 20 minutes.

3 Mix the vinegar, soy sauce and sugar in a bowl.

4 Remove the chicken from the egg white mixture.

5 Heat the oil in a preheated wok, add the chicken and stir fry for 3–4 minutes, until golden brown. Remove the chicken from the wok with a slotted spoon, set aside and keep warm.

6

7

6 Add the garlic, ginger root, bell pepper, and mushrooms to the wok and stir-fry for 1–2 minutes.

7 Add the yellow bean sauce and cook for 1 minute. Stir in the vinegar mixture and return the chicken to the wok. Cook for 1–2 minutes and serve hot, garnished with bell pepper strips.

stir-fried chicken strips & golden rice

This is a really colorful main meal or side dish which tastes just
as good as it looks. Cook the vegetables quickly to keep them crispy.

Serves 4

1¾ cups long-grain white rice

1 tsp turmeric

2 tbsp sunflower oil

12 oz skinless, boneless chicken breasts
  or thighs, sliced

1 red bell pepper, deseeded and sliced

1 green bell pepper, deseeded and sliced

1 green chile, deseeded and finely chopped

1 medium carrot, coarsely grated

1½ cups beansprouts

6 scallions, sliced, plus extra to garnish
  (optional)

2 tbsp soy sauce

1

4

7

1 Place the rice and turmeric in a
large pan of lightly salted water and
cook until the grains of rice are just
tender, about 10 minutes. Drain the rice
thoroughly and press out any excess
water with double thickness paper
towels.

2 Heat the sunflower oil in a large
preheated wok.

3 Add the strips of chicken to the
wok and stir-fry over a high heat
until the chicken is just beginning to turn
a golden colour.

4 Add the bell peppers and chile to
the wok and stir-fry for 2–3 minutes.

5 Add the rice to the wok, a little at
a time, tossing well after each
addition until well combined.

6 Add the carrot, beansprouts and
scallions to the wok and stir-fry for a
further 2 minutes.

7 Drizzle with the soy sauce and
mix well.

8 Garnish with extra scallions, if
wished and serve at once.

variation

Use pork marinated in hoisin
sauce instead of the chicken,
if you prefer.

fiery chicken & sherry stir-fry

This is quite a hot dish, using fresh chiles. If you prefer a milder dish, halve the number of chiles used.

Serves 4

12 oz skinless, boneless lean chicken

½ tsp salt

1 egg white, lightly beaten

2 tbsp cornstarch

4 tbsp vegetable oil

2 garlic cloves, crushed

½ inch piece fresh ginger root grated

1 red bell pepper, seeded and diced

1 green bell pepper, seeded and diced

2 fresh red chiles, chopped

2 tbsp light soy sauce

1 tbsp dry sherry or Chinese rice wine

1 tbsp wine vinegar

1 Cut the chicken into cubes and place in a mixing bowl. Add the salt, egg white, cornstarch and 1 tablespoon of the oil. Turn the chicken in the mixture to coat thoroughly.

2 Heat the remaining oil in a preheated wok. Add the garlic and ginger root and stir-fry for 30 seconds.

3 Add the chicken pieces to the wok and stir-fry for 2–3 minutes, or until browned.

4 Stir in the bell peppers, chiles, soy sauce, sherry or Chinese rice wine, and wine vinegar and cook for a further 2–3 minutes, until the chicken is cooked through. Transfer to a warm serving dish and serve.

4

1

3

variation

This recipe works well if you use 12 oz lean steak, cut into thin strips or 1 lb raw shrimp instead of the chicken.

cook's tip

When preparing chiles, wear rubber gloves to prevent the juices from burning and irritating your hands. Be careful not to touch your face, especially your lips or eyes until you have washed your hands.

buttered chicken

A simple and mouthwatering dish with a lovely thick sauce, this makes an impressive centerpiece for a dinner party.

Serves 4-6

8 tbsp sweet butter

1 tbsp oil

2 medium onions, finely chopped

1 tsp fresh ginger root, finely chopped

2 tsp garam masala

2 tsp ground coriander

1 tsp chili powder

1 tsp black cumin seeds

1 tsp fresh garlic, crushed

1 tsp salt

3 whole green cardamoms

3 whole black peppercorns

⅔ cup natural yogurt

2 tbsp tomato paste

8 chicken pieces, skinned

⅔ cup water

2 whole bay leaves

⅔ cup light cream

fresh cilantro leaves and green chiles,
    chopped, to garnish

2

2

1 Heat the butter and oil in a large
  skillet. Add the onions and sauté
until golden brown, stirring. Reduce
the heat.

2 Crush the fresh ginger root and
  place in a bowl. Add the garam
masala, ground coriander, chili powder,
black cumin seeds, garlic, salt,
cardamoms and black peppercorns and
blend. Add the yogurt and tomato paste
and stir to combine.

3 Add the chicken pieces to the
  yogurt and spice mixture and mix to
coat well.

4 Add the chicken to the onions in
  the pan and stir-fry vigorously,
making semi-circular movements, for
5—7 minutes.

5 Add the water and the bay leaves
  to the mixture in the pan and leave
to simmer for 30 minutes, stirring
occasionally.

6 Add the cream and cook for
  a further 10—15 minutes.

7 Garnish with fresh cilantro leaves
  and chilies and serve hot.

2

chicken tossed in black pepper

Using black pepper instead of chili powder produces a milder curry. This recipe is basically a stir-fry and can be prepared in a short time. The dish goes well with fried corn and peas.

Serves 4-6

8 chicken thighs

1 tsp fresh ginger root, finely chopped

1 tsp fresh garlic, crushed

1 tsp salt

1½ tsp pepper

⅔ cup oil

1 green bell pepper, roughly sliced

⅔ cup water

2 tbsp lemon juice

FRIED CORN & PEAS

2 oz sweet butter

8 oz frozen corn

8 oz frozen peas

½ tsp salt

½ tsp chili powder

1 tbsp lemon juice

fresh cilantro leaves, to garnish

1

2

6

1 Using a sharp knife, bone the chicken thighs, if you prefer.

2 Combine the ginger root, garlic, salt and black pepper together in a mixing bowl.

3 Add the chicken pieces to the black pepper mixture and set aside until required.

4 Heat the oil in a large pan. Add the chicken pieces and stir-fry for 10 minutes.

5 Reduce the heat and add the green bell pepper and the water to the pan. Leave the mixture to simmer for 10 minutes, then sprinkle over the lemon juice.

6 Meanwhile, make the fried corn and peas. Melt the butter in a large skillet. Add the corn and peas and sauté, stirring occasionally, for about 10 minutes. Add the salt and chili powder and sauté for a further 5 minutes.

7 Sprinkle over the lemon juice and garnish with fresh cilantro leaves.

8 Transfer the chicken and bell pepper mixture to serving plates and serve with the fried corn and peas.

indonesian potato & chicken salad

The spicy peanut dressing served with this salad may be prepared in advance and left to chill a day before required.

Serves 4

4 large waxy potatoes, diced

10½ oz fresh pineapple, diced

2 carrots, grated

6 oz beansprouts

1 bunch scallions, sliced

1 large zucchini, cut into matchsticks

3 celery stalks, cut into matchsticks

6 oz unsalted peanuts

2 cooked chicken breast fillets,
    about 4½ oz each, sliced

DRESSING

6 tbsp crunchy peanut butter

6 tbsp olive oil

2 tbsp light soy sauce

1 red chile, chopped

2 tsp sesame oil

4 tsp lime juice

lime wedges, to garnish

3

4

5

1 Cook the diced potatoes in a pan of boiling water for 10 minutes or until tender. Drain and leave to cool.

2 Transfer the cooled potatoes to a salad bowl.

3 Add the pineapple, carrots, beansprouts, scallions, zucchini, celery, peanuts, and sliced chicken to the potatoes. Toss well to mix all the salad ingredients together.

4 To make the dressing, put the peanut butter in a small bowl and gradually whisk in the olive oil and light soy sauce.

5 Stir in the chopped red chile, sesame oil, and lime juice. Mix until well combined.

cook's tip

Unsweetened canned pineapple may be used in place of the fresh pineapple for convenience. If only sweetened canned pineapple is available, drain it and rinse under cold running water before using.

6 Pour the spicy dressing over the salad and toss lightly to coat all of the ingredients. Serve the salad immediately, garnished with lime wedges.

spicy peanut chicken

This quick dish has many variations, but this version includes the classic combination of peanuts, chicken, and chiles, blending together to give a wonderfully flavored dish.

Serves 4

2 oz skinless, boneless chicken breast

2 tbsp peanut oil

1 cup shelled peanuts

1 fresh red chile, sliced

1 green bell pepper, seeded and cut into strips

fried rice, to serve

SAUCE

⅔ cup chicken bouillon

1 tbsp Chinese rice wine or dry sherry

1 tbsp light soy sauce

1½ tsp light brown sugar

2 garlic cloves, finely chopped

1 tsp grated fresh ginger root

1 tsp rice wine vinegar

1 tsp sesame oil

1 Trim any fat from the chicken and cut the meat into 1 inch cubes. Set aside.

2 Heat the peanut oil in a preheated wok. Add the peanuts and stir-fry for 1 minute. Remove the peanuts with a slotted spoon and set aside.

3 Add the chicken to the wok and cook for 1–2 minutes. Stir in the chili and green bell pepper and cook for 1 minute. Remove from the wok with a slotted spoon and set aside.

4 Put half of the peanuts in a food processor and process until almost smooth. Alternatively, place them in a plastic bag and crush them with a rolling pin.

5 To make the sauce, add the chicken bouillon, Chinese rice wine or dry sherry, soy sauce, sugar, garlic, ginger root, and rice wine vinegar to the wok.

6 Heat the sauce without boiling and stir in the peanuts, chicken, chile, and bell pepper.

7 Sprinkle the sesame oil into the wok, stir and cook for 1 minute. Serve hot with fried rice.

cook's tip

If necessary, process the peanuts with a little of the bouillon in step 4 to form a softer paste.

3

4

6

prosciutto-wrapped chicken

There is a delicious surprise inside these chicken breast parcels!

Serves 4

4 chicken breasts, skin removed

3½ oz full fat soft cheese, flavored with
    herbs and garlic

8 slices prosciutto

⅔ cup red wine

⅔ cup chicken bouillon

1 tbsp brown sugar

variation

Try adding 2 finely chopped
sun-dried tomatoes to the soft
cheese in step 2, if you
prefer.

1

2

3

4 Pour the wine and chicken bouillon into a large skillet and bring to the boil. When the mixture is just starting to boil, add the sugar and stir to dissolve.

5 Add the chicken breasts to the mixture in the skillet. Leave to simmer for 12–15 minutes or the chicken is tender and the juices run clear when a skewer is inserted into the thickest part of the meat.

6 Remove the chicken from the pan, set aside and keep warm.

7 Reheat the sauce and boil until reduced and thickened. Remove the string from the chicken and cut into slices. Pour the sauce over the chicken to serve.

1 Using a sharp knife, make a horizontal slit along the length of each chicken breast to form a pocket.

2 Beat the cheese with a wooden spoon to soften it. Spoon the cheese into the pocket of the chicken breasts.

3 Wrap 2 slices of prosciutto around each chicken breast and secure in place with a length of string.

chicken in red bell pepper & almond sauce

This tasty chicken dish combines warm spices and almonds and is spiked with anise to produce an exotic mix of flavors.

Serves 4

2 tbsp butter

7 tbsp vegetable oil

4 skinless, boneless chicken breasts,
    cut into 2 inch x 1 inch pieces

1 medium onion, roughly chopped

1 inch piece fresh ginger root

3 garlic cloves, peeled

¼ cup blanched almonds

1 large red bell pepper, roughly chopped

1 tbsp ground cumin

2 tsp ground coriander

1 tsp ground turmeric

pinch cayenne pepper

½ tsp salt

⅔ cup water

3 star anise

2 tbsp lemon juice

pepper

slivered almonds, to garnish

rice, to serve

1

1 Heat the butter and
1 tablespoon of oil in a skillet, add the chicken pieces and cook for 5 minutes until golden. Transfer the chicken pieces to a plate and keep warm until required.

2 Combine the onion, ginger root, garlic, almonds, red bell pepper, cumin, coriander, turmeric, cayenne pepper, and salt in a food processor or liquidiser. Blend to form a smooth paste.

3 Heat the remaining oil in a large pan or deep skillet. Add the paste and sauté for 10–12 minutes.

4 Add the chicken pieces, the water, star anise, lemon juice and pepper. Cover, reduce the heat and simmer gently for 25 minutes or until the chicken is tender, stirring a few times during cooking.

5 Transfer the chicken to a serving dish, sprinkle with the slivered almonds and serve with individual rice moulds.

2

4

kashmiri chicken

This warming, rich, and spicy dish is based on the traditional cooking style of Northern India, using chicken on the bone.

Serves 4

4 skinless chicken drumsticks

4 skinless chicken thighs

⅔ cup unsweetened yogurt

4 tbsp Tikka curry paste

2 tbsp sunflower oil

1 medium onion, sliced thinly

1 garlic clove, crushed

1 tsp ground cumin

1 tsp finely chopped fresh ginger root

½ tsp chili paste

4 tsp chicken bouillon

2 tbsp ground almonds

salt

fresh cilantro, to garnish

pilau rice, pickles, and poppadums, to serve

variation

If you prefer, use boneless chicken breasts instead of legs, and cut into large chunks for cooking.

2

1 Slash the chicken fairly deeply at intervals with a sharp knife and place in a large bowl.

2 Mix together the unsweetened yogurt and curry paste and stir into the chicken, tossing to coat evenly. Cover and chill for at least 1 hour.

3 Heat the oil in a large pan and sauté the onion and garlic for 4–5 minutes until softened but not browned.

4 Stir in the cumin, ginger root, and chili paste and cook gently for 1 minute.

5 Add the chicken pieces and cook gently, turning from time to time, for about 10 minutes or until evenly browned. Stir in any remaining marinade with the bouillon and almonds.

6 Cover the pan and simmer gently for a further 15 minutes or until the chicken is completely cooked and tender.

7 Season to taste with a little salt. Garnish the chicken with cilantro and serve with pilau rice, pickles, and poppadums.

3

4

spicy chicken tortillas

Serve these easy-to-prepare tortillas to friends or as a special family supper. The chicken filling has a mild, mellow spicy heat and a fresh salad makes a perfect accompaniment.

Serves 4

2 tbsp oil

8 skinless, boneless chicken thighs, sliced

1 onion, chopped

2 garlic cloves, chopped

1 tsp cumin seeds, roughly crushed

2 large dried chilies, sliced

14 oz can tomatoes

14 oz can red kidney beans, drained

⅔ cup chicken bouillon

2 tsp sugar

salt and pepper

TO SERVE

1 large ripe avocado

1 lime

8 soft tortillas

1 cup thick yogurt

lime wedges, to garnish

variation

For a vegetarian filling, replace the chicken with 14 oz canned pinto or cannellini beans and use vegetable bouillon instead of the chicken bouillon.

1

2

3

1 Heat the oil in a large skillet or wok, add the chicken and sauté for 3 minutes until golden. Add the onion and sauté for 5 minutes, stirring until browned. Add the garlic, cumin, and chilies, with their seeds, and cook for about 1 minute.

2 Add the tomatoes, kidney beans, bouillon, sugar, and salt and pepper to taste. Bring to a boil, breaking up the tomatoes. Cover and simmer for 15 minutes. Remove the lid and cook for 5 minutes, stirring occasionally until the sauce has thickened.

3 Halve the avocado, discard the stone and scoop out the flesh on to a plate. Mash the avocado with a fork. Cut half of the lime into 8 thin wedges. Squeeze the juice from the remaining lime over the avocado.

4 Warm the tortillas following the instructions on the packet. Put 2 tortillas on each serving plate, fill with the chicken mixture and top with spoonfuls of avocado and yogurt. Garnish the tortillas with lime wedges.

chicken & onions

This dish represents one of the rare occasions when we do not use yogurt to cook chicken. It has a lovely flavor and is perfect served with rice. It also freezes very well.

Serves 4

1¼ cups oil

4 medium onions, finely chopped

1½ tsp fresh ginger root, finely chopped

1½ tsp garam masala

1½ tsp fresh garlic, crushed

1 tsp chili powder

1 tsp ground coriander

3 whole cardamoms

3 peppercorns

3 tbsp tomato paste

8 chicken thighs, skinned

1¼ cups water

2 tbsp lemon juice

1 green chile

fresh cilantro leaves

green chili strips, to garnish

1

3

4

1 Heat the oil in a large skillet. Add the onions, and sauté, stirring occasionally, until golden brown.

2 Reduce the heat and add the ginger root, garam masala, garlic, chili powder, ground coriander, whole cardamoms, and the peppercorns, stirring to mix.

3 Add the tomato paste to the mixture in the skillet and stir-fry for 5–7 minutes.

4 Add the chicken thighs to the pan and toss to coat with the spice mixture.

5 Add the water, cover and leave to simmer for 20–25 minutes.

6 Add the lemon juice, green chile, and cilantro to the mixture, and combine.

7 Transfer the chicken and onions to serving plates, garnish and serve hot.

cook's tip

A dish of meat cooked with plenty of onions is called a Do Pyaza. This curry definitely improves if made in advance and then reheated before serving. This develops the flavors and makes them deeper.

chicken with a curried yogurt crust

A spicy, Indian-style coating is baked around lean chicken to give a full flavor. Serve hot or cold with a tomato, cucumber, and cilantro relish.

Serves 4

1 garlic clove, finely chopped

1 inch piece ginger root, finely chopped

1 fresh green chile, deseeded and finely chopped

6 tbsp low-fat unsweetened yogurt

1 tbsp tomato paste

1 tsp ground turmeric

1 tsp garam masala

1 tbsp lime juice

salt and pepper

4 boneless, skinless chicken breasts, each 4½ oz

wedges of lime or lemon, to serve

RELISH

4 medium tomatoes

¼ cucumber

1 small red onion

2 tbsp fresh cilantro, chopped

variation

The spicy yogurt coating would work just as well if spread on a chunky white fish such as cod fillet. The cooking time should be reduced to 15–20 minutes.

1

2

1 Preheat the oven to 375°F. In a small bowl mix together the garlic, ginger root, chili, yogurt, tomato paste, turmeric, garam masala, lime juice, and seasoning.

2 Wash and pat dry the chicken breasts and place them on a baking sheet. Brush or spread the spicy yogurt mix over the chicken, and bake in the oven for 30–35 minutes until the meat is tender and cooked through.

3 Meanwhile, make the relish. Finely chop the tomatoes, cucumber, and onion and mix together with the cilantro. Season, cover and chill until required.

4 Drain the cooked chicken on absorbent kitchen paper and serve hot with the relish. Or, allow to cool, chill for at least 1 hour and serve sliced as part of a salad.

3

spanish chicken with shrimp

This unusual dish, with its mixture of chicken and shellfish, is typically Spanish. The basis of this recipe is sofrito: a slow-cooked mixture of onion and tomato in olive oil, with garlic and peppers.

Serves 4

4 chicken quarters

1 tbsp olive oil

1 red bell pepper

1 medium onion

2 garlic cloves, crushed

14 oz can chopped tomatoes

scant 1 cup dry white wine

4 tbsp chopped fresh oregano

salt and pepper

1 cup chorizo sausage

1 cup peeled shrimp

rice, to serve

cook's tip

Chorizo is a spicy Spanish sausage made with pork and a hot pepper such as cayenne or pimento. It is available from large stores and specialist butchers.

1

2

1 Remove the skin from the chicken quarters. Heat the oil in a wide, heavy pan and sauté the chicken, turning occasionally until golden brown.

2 Using a sharp knife, seed and slice the bell pepper and peel and slice the onion. Add the bell pepper and onion to the pan and sauté gently to soften.

4

3 Add the garlic with the tomatoes, wine and oregano. Season well with salt and pepper, then bring to a boil, cover and simmer gently for 45 minutes or until the chicken is tender and the juices run clear when the thickest part of the chicken is pierced with a skewer.

4 Thinly slice the chorizo and add to the pan together with the shrimp, then simmer for a further 5 minutes. Adjust the seasoning to taste and serve with rice.

caribbean chicken

This exotic dish can be made with any cut of chicken, but drumsticks are best for quick and even cooking. Grated fresh coconut adds a delicious, tropical flavor.

Serves 4

8 skinless chicken drumsticks

2 limes

1 tsp cayenne pepper

2 medium mangoes

1 tbsp sunflower oil

2 tbsp dark brown sugar

2 tbsp coarsely grated coconut,
   to serve (optional)

lime wedges and fresh parsley,
   to garnish

1 With a sharp knife, slash the
chicken drumsticks at intervals then
place the chicken in a large bowl.

2 Grate the rind from the limes
and set aside.

3 Squeeze the juice from the limes
and sprinkle over the chicken with
the cayenne pepper. Cover and chill in
the refrigerator for at least two hours
or overnight.

4 Peel the mangoes and chop in half.
Discard the stone and cut the flesh
into slices.

3

4

5 Drain the chicken drumsticks using
a draining spoon and reserve the
juice. Heat the oil in a wide heavy pan
and sauté the chicken drumsticks,
turning frequently, until golden. Stir in the
marinade, lime rind, mango slices, and
the dark brown sugar.

6 Cover the pan and simmer gently,
stirring occasionally, for 15 minutes,
or until the chicken juices run clear when
pierced with a skewer. Sprinkle with
grated coconut, if using, and garnish
with lime wedges and fresh parsley.

5

cook's tip

When buying mangoes, bear in
mind that the skin of ripe
mangoes varies in color from
green to pinky-red and the
flesh from pale yellow to
bright orange. Choose mangoes
which yield to gentle
pressure.

cumin-spiced apricot chicken

Spiced chicken legs are partially boned and packed with dried apricots for an intense fruity flavor. A golden, spiced, low-fat yogurt coating keeps the chicken moist and tender.

Serves 4

4 large, skinless chicken leg quarters

finely grated rind of 1 lemon

salt, pepper

1 cup ready-to-eat dried apricots

1 tbsp ground cumin

1 tsp ground turmeric

½ cup low-fat unsweetened yogurt

1½ cups brown rice

2 tbsp slivered hazelnuts
   or almonds, toasted

2 tbsp sunflower seeds, toasted

lemon wedges and a fresh salad, to serve

1 Remove any excess fat from the chicken legs.

2 Use a small sharp knife carefully to cut the flesh away from the thigh bone.

3 Scrape the meat away down as far as the knuckle. Grasp the thigh bone firmly and twist it to break it away from the drumstick.

4 Open out the boned part of the chicken and sprinkle with lemon rind and pepper. Pack the dried apricots into each piece of chicken. Fold over to enclose, and secure with toothpicks.

5 Mix together the cumin, turmeric, yogurt, and salt and pepper, then brush this mixture over the chicken to coat evenly. Place the chicken in an ovenproof dish or roasting pan and bake in a preheated oven, 375°F, for about 35–40 minutes, or until the juices run clear, not pink, when the chicken is pierced through the thickest part with a skewer.

6 Meanwhile, cook the rice in boiling, lightly salted water until just tender, then drain well. Stir the hazelnuts or almonds and sunflower seeds into the rice. Serve the chicken with the nutty rice, lemon wedges, and a fresh salad.

tandoori-style chicken

In India, tandoori chicken is traditionally cooked in a tandoor (clay) oven.
Alternatively, you can pre-heat the broiler to a very high temperature then
lower it to medium to cook this dish.

Serves 4

8 chicken drumsticks, skinned

⅔ cup unsweetened yogurt

1½ tsp fresh ginger root, finely chopped

1½ tsp fresh garlic, finely chopped

1 tsp chili powder

2 tsp ground cumin

2 tsp ground coriander

1 tsp salt

½ tsp red food colouring

1 tbsp tamarind paste

⅔ cup water

⅔ cup oil

lettuce leaves, to serve

onion rings, sliced tomatoes, and lemon
     wedges, to garnish

cook's tip

Serve the succulent chicken pieces on a bed of lettuce, and garnished with a few onion rings, sliced tomatoes and lemon wedges. Shop-bought naan bread and raita will complement the dish perfectly.

2

1 Make 2-3 slashes in each piece of chicken.

2 Place the yogurt in a bowl. Add the ginger root, garlic, chili powder, ground cumin, ground coriander, salt, and red food colouring and blend together until well combined.

3 Add the chicken to the yogurt and spice mixture and mix to coat well. Leave the chicken to marinate in the refrigerator for a minimum of 3 hours.

4 In a separate bowl, mix the tamarind paste with the water and fold into the yogurt and spice mixture. Toss the chicken pieces in this mixture and set aside to marinate for a further 3 hours.

5 Transfer the chicken pieces to a heatproof dish and brush the chicken with oil. Cook the chicken under a pre-heated medium-hot broiler for 30–35 minutes, turning the chicken pieces occasionally and basting with the remaining oil.

6 Arrange the chicken on a bed of lettuce and garnish with onion rings, sliced tomatoes and lemon wedges.

3

5

cajun chicken gumbo

This complete main course is cooked in one saucepan for simplicity. If you're cooking for one, simply halve the ingredients; the cooking time should stay the same.

Serves 2

1 tbsp sunflower oil

4 chicken thighs

1 small onion, diced

2 stalks celery, diced

1 small green bell pepper, diced

½ cup long grain rice

1¼ cups chicken bouillon

1 small red chile

9 oz okra

1 tbsp tomato paste

salt and pepper

1 Heat the oil in a wide pan and sauté the chicken until golden. Remove the chicken from the pan using a draining spoon. Stir in the onion, celery, and bell pepper and sauté for 1 minute. Pour off any excess fat.

2 Add the rice and sauté, stirring briskly, for a further minute. Add the chicken bouillon and heat until boiling.

3 Thinly slice the chile and trim the okra. Add to the pan with the tomato paste. Season to taste.

4 Return the chicken to the pan and stir. Cover tightly and simmer gently for 15 minutes, or until the rice is tender, the chicken is thoroughly cooked and all the liquid absorbed. Stir occasionally and if the gumbo becomes too dry, add a little extra bouillon to moisten. Serve immediately.

4

2

3

cook's tip

The whole chile makes the dish hot and spicy—if you prefer a milder flavour, discard the seeds of the chile.

variation

You can replace the chicken with 9 oz peeled shrimp and 3 oz belly of pork, if desired. Slice the pork and sauté in the oil before adding the onions, and add the shrimp 5 minutes before the end of cooking time.

thai stir-fried chicken with vegetables

Coconut adds a creamy texture and delicious flavor to this Thai-style stir-fry, which is spiked with green chile.

2

Serves 4

3 tbsp sesame oil

12 oz chicken breast, sliced thinly

salt and pepper

8 shallots, sliced

2 garlic cloves, finely chopped

1 inch piece fresh ginger root, grated

1 green chile, finely chopped

1 each red and green bell pepper,
   sliced thinly

3 zucchini, thinly sliced

2 tbsp ground almonds

1 tsp ground cinnamon

1 tbsp oyster sauce

¼ cup creamed coconut, grated

3

1 Heat the sesame oil in a wok, add
  the chicken, season with salt and
pepper, and stir fry for about 4 minutes.

2 Add the shallots, garlic, ginger root,
  and chile and stir-fry for 2 minutes.

3 Add the bell peppers and zucchini
  and cook for about 1 minute.

4 Finally, add the remaining
  ingredients. Stir-fry for 1 minute
and serve.

4

cook's tip

Creamed coconut is sold in
blocks by stores. It is a
useful pantry standby as it
adds richness and depth of
flavour.

cook's tip

Since most of the heat of
chilies comes from the seeds,
remove them before cooking if
you want a milder flavour.
Be very careful when handling
chiles—do not touch your
face or eyes as the chile
juice can be very painful.
Always wash your hands after
preparing chiles.

chicken jalfrezi

This is a quick and tasty way to use leftover roast chicken. The sauce can also be used for any cooked poultry, lamb, or beef.

Serves 4

1 tsp mustard oil

3 tbsp vegetable oil

1 large onion, chopped finely

3 garlic cloves, crushed

1 tbsp tomato paste

2 tomatoes, peeled and chopped

1 tsp ground turmeric

½ tsp cumin seeds, ground

½ tsp coriander seeds, ground

½ tsp chili powder

½ tsp garam masala

1 tsp red wine vinegar

1 small red bell pepper, chopped

1 cup frozen fava beans

1 lb cooked chicken breasts,
   cut into bite-sized pieces

salt

fresh cilantro sprigs, to garnish

1 Heat the mustard oil in a large, skillet set over a high heat for about 1 minute until it begins to smoke. Add the vegetable oil, reduce the heat and then add the onion and the garlic. Sauté the garlic and onion until they are golden.

2 Add the tomato paste, chopped tomatoes, ground turmeric, cumin and coriander seeds, chili powder, garam masala, and red wine vinegar to the skillet. Stir the mixture until fragrant.

3 Add the red bell pepper and fava beans and stir for 2 minutes until the bell pepper is softened. Stir in the chicken, and salt to taste. Leave to simmer gently for 6–8 minutes until the chicken is heated through and the beans are tender.

2

3

4 Serve garnished with cilantro leaves.

cook's tip

This dish is an ideal way of making use of leftover poultry—turkey, duck, or quail. Any variety of beans works well, but vegetables are just as useful, especially root vegetables, zucchini, potatoes, or broccoli. Leafy vegetables will not be so successful.

1

chile chicken & corn meatballs

Tender chicken nuggets are served with a sweet and sour sauce that is packed full of flavor, yet simple to prepare.

Serves 4

1 lb lean chicken, ground

4 scallions, trimmed and finely chopped

1 small red chile, seeded and finely chopped

salt and white pepper

1 inch piece ginger root, finely chopped

3½ oz canned corn (no added sugar or salt),
    drained

⅔ cup fresh chicken bouillon

3½ oz cubed pineapple in natural juice,
    drained, with 4 tbsp reserved juice

1 medium carrot, cut into thin strips

1 small red bell pepper, seeded and diced

1 small green bell pepper, seeded and diced

1 tbsp light soy sauce

2 tbsp rice vinegar

1 tbsp superfine sugar

1 tbsp tomato paste

2 tsp cornstarch mixed to a paste with
    4 tsp cold water

boiled jasmine rice, to serve

chives, snipped, to garnish

2

2

1 To make the meatballs, place the chicken in a bowl and add the scallion, chile, ginger root, seasoning, and corn. Mix together with your hands.

2 Divide the mixture into 16 portions and form each into a ball. Bring a saucepan of water to a boil. Arrange the meatballs on a sheet of baking parchment in a steamer or large strainer, place over the water, cover and steam for 10–12 minutes.

3 To make the sauce, pour the bouillon and pineapple juice into a saucepan and bring to the boil. Add the carrot and bell peppers, cover and simmer for 5 minutes.

3

4 Stir in the remaining ingredients and heat through, stirring, until thickened. Season and set aside until required.

5 Drain the meatballs and transfer to a serving plate. Garnish with snipped chives and serve with boiled jasmine rice and the sauce (reheated if necessary).

teppanyaki

This simple, Japanese style of cooking is ideal for thinly sliced breast of chicken. Mirin is a rich, sweet rice wine which is available from Asian shops.

Serves 4

4 boneless chicken breasts

1 red bell pepper

1 green bell pepper

4 scallions

8 baby corn

½ cup beansprouts

1 tbsp sesame or sunflower oil

4 tbsp soy sauce

4 tbsp mirin

1 tbsp grated fresh ginger root

cook's tip

If you cannot find mirin add 1 tbsp of soft, light brown sugar to the sauce instead.

variation

Instead of serving the sauce as a dip, you could use it as a marinade. However, do not leave it to marinate for more than 2 hours as the soy sauce will cause the chicken to dry out and become tough. Use other vegetables, such as snow peas or thinly sliced carrots, if you prefer.

1

2

1 Remove the skin from the chicken and slice at a slight angle, to a thickness of about ¼ inch.

2 Seed and thinly slice the bell peppers and trim and slice the scallions and corn. Arrange the bell peppers, scallions, corn, and beansprouts on a plate with the sliced chicken.

3 Heat a large griddle or heavy skillet then lightly brush with oil. Add the vegetables and chicken slices in small batches, allowing space between them so they cook thoroughly.

4 In a small bowl, mix together the soy sauce, mirin, and ginger root and serve as a dip with the chicken and vegetables.

4

mexican chicken

Chile, tomatoes, and corn are typical ingredients in a Mexican dish.

Serves 4

2 tbsp oil

8 chicken drumsticks

1 medium onion, finely chopped

1 tsp chili powder

1 tsp ground coriander

14 oz can chopped tomatoes

2 tbsp tomato paste

⅔ cup frozen corn

salt and pepper

rice and mixed bell pepper salad, to serve

cook's tip

Mexican dishes are not usually suitable for freezing because the strong flavors they contain, such as chile, intensify during freezing, and if left for too long, an unpleasant, musty flavour can develop.

1 Heat the oil in a large skillet, add the chicken drumsticks and cook over a medium heat until lightly browned. Remove the chicken drumsticks from the pan with a draining spoon and set aside until required.

2 Add the chopped onion to the pan and cook for 3–4 minutes until softened, then stir in the chili powder and coriander and cook for a few seconds, stirring briskly so the spices do not burn on the bottom of the pan. Add the chopped tomatoes with their juice and the tomato paste and stir well to incorporate.

3 Return the chicken drumsticks to the pan and simmer the casserole gently for 20 minutes until the chicken is tender and thoroughly cooked. Add the corn and cook for a further 3–4 minutes. Season with salt and pepper to taste.

4 Serve with rice and mixed bell pepper salad.

chicken chow mein

This classic dish requires no introduction as it is already a favorite amongst most Chinese food-eaters and is familiar to almost everybody.

Serves 4

9 oz packet of medium egg noodles

2 tbsp sunflower oil

9½ oz cooked chicken breasts, shredded

1 clove garlic, finely chopped

1 red bell pepper, seeded and thinly sliced

3½ oz shiitake mushrooms, sliced

6 scallions, sliced

1 cup beansprouts

3 tbsp soy sauce

1 tbsp sesame oil

1

5

4

1 Place the egg noodles in a large bowl or dish and break them up slightly.

2 Pour enough boiling water over the noodles to cover and leave to stand whilst preparing the other ingredients.

3 Heat the sunflower oil in a large preheated wok.

4 Add the shredded chicken, finely chopped garlic, bell pepper slices, mushrooms, scallions, and beansprouts to the wok and stir–fry for about 5 minutes.

5 Drain the noodles thoroughly. Add the noodles to the wok, toss well and stir–fry for a further 5 minutes.

6 Drizzle the soy sauce and sesame oil over the chow mein and toss until well combined.

7 Transfer the chicken chow mein to warm serving bowls and serve immediately.

variation

You can make the chow mein with a selection of vegetables for a vegetarian dish, if you prefer.

lemon chicken

This is on everyone's list of favorite Chinese dishes, and it is so simple to make. Fried chicken is cooked in a tangy lemon sauce in minutes and is great served with stir-fried vegetables.

3

4

Serves 4

vegetable oil, for deep–frying

1½ lb skinless, boneless chicken,
   cut into strips

1 tbsp cornstarch

6 tbsp cold water

3 tbsp fresh lemon juice

2 tbsp sweet sherry

½ tsp superfine sugar

lemon slices and shredded scallion,
   to garnish

---

cook's tip

If you would prefer to use
chicken portions rather than
strips, cook them in the oil,
covered, over a low heat for
about 30 minutes, or until
cooked through.

---

1 Heat the oil in a preheated wok until almost smoking. Reduce the heat and stir–fry the chicken strips for 3–4 minutes, until cooked through. Remove the chicken with a draining spoon, set aside and keep warm. Drain the oil from the wok.

2 To make the sauce, mix the cornstarch with 2 tablespoons of the water to form a paste.

3 Pour the lemon juice and remaining water into the mixture in the wok. Add the sherry and sugar and bring to the boil, stirring until the sugar has completely dissolved.

4 Stir in the cornflour mixture and return to a boil. Reduce the heat and simmer, stirring constantly, for 2–3 minutes, until the sauce is thickened and clear.

5 Transfer the chicken to a warm serving plate and pour the sauce over the top. Garnish with the lemon slices and shredded scallion and serve immediately.

1

fruity garlic curried chicken

Serve this fruity curry with mango chutney and naan bread, and top the curry with pitless grapes. Mangoes or pears make a good substitute for pineapple.

Serves 4-6

1 tbsp oil

2 lb chicken meat, chopped

4 tbsp all-purpose flour, seasoned

32 shallots, roughly chopped

4 garlic cloves, finely chopped with
   a little olive oil

3 cooking apples, diced

1 pineapple, diced

¾ cup golden raisins

1 tbsp clear honey

1¼ cups chicken bouillon

2 tbsp Worcestershire sauce

3 tbsp hot curry paste

salt and pepper

⅔ cup sour cream

rice, to serve

orange slices, to garnish

1 Heat the oil in a large skillet. Coat the meat in the seasoned flour and cook for about 4 minutes until it is browned all over. Transfer the chicken to a large deep casserole and keep warm until required.

2 Slowly sauté the shallots, garlic, apples, pineapple, and golden raisins in the pan juices.

3 Add the honey, chicken bouillon, Worcestershire sauce, and hot curry paste. Season to taste with salt and pepper.

4 Pour the sauce over the chicken and cover the casserole with a lid or cooking foil.

5 Cook in the center of a preheated oven, 350°F, for about 2 hours. Stir in the sour cream and cook for a further 15 minutes. Serve the curry with rice, garnished with a slice of orange.

variation

Coconut rice also makes an excellent accompaniment to this dish. Place 1 oz chopped creamed coconut, 1 cinnamon stick, 2¼ cups water in a large pan and bring to the boil. Stir in 1¾ cups basmati rice, cover and simmer gently for 15 minutes until all the liquid has been absorbed. Remove the cinnamon stick before serving.

2   3   5

spicy roast chicken

This chicken dish, ideal for dinner parties, is cooked in the oven—which is very rare in Indian cooking. The chicken can be boned, if desired.

Serves 4

¼ cup ground almonds

⅓ cup shredded coconut

⅔ cup oil

1 medium onion, finely chopped

1 tsp fresh ginger root, chopped

1 tsp fresh garlic, crushed

1 tsp chili powder

1½ tsp garam masala

1 tsp salt

⅔ cup yogurt

4 chicken quarters, skinned

green salad leaves, to serve

fresh cilantro leaves, and 1 lemon, cut into
    wedges, to garnish

1 In a heavy–based pan, dry roast the ground almonds and coconut and set aside.

2 Heat the oil in a skillet and sauté the onion, stirring, until golden brown.

1

3

5

3 Place the ginger root, garlic, chili powder, garam masala, and salt in a bowl and mix with the yogurt. Add the almonds and coconut and mix well.

4 Add the onions to the spice mixture, blend and set aside.

5 Arrange the chicken quarters in the bottom of a heatproof dish. Spoon the spice mixture over the chicken sparingly.

6 Cook in a pre–heated oven, 425°F, for 35–45 minutes. Check that the chicken is cooked thoroughly by piercing the thickest part of the meat with a sharp knife or a fine skewer—the juices will run clear when the chicken is cooked through. Garnish with the cilantro and lemon wedges and serve with a salad.

cook's tip

If you want a spicier dish, add more chili powder and garam masala.

golden chicken pilau

This is a simple version of a creamy textured and mildly spiced Indian pilau. Although there are lots of ingredients, there's very little preparation needed for this dish.

Serves 4

4 tbsp butter

8 skinless, boneless chicken thighs,
    cut into large pieces

1 medium onion, sliced

1 tsp ground turmeric

1 tsp ground cinnamon

1 cup long–grain rice

salt and pepper

1¾ cups unsweetened yogurt

⅓ cup golden raisins

1 scant cup chicken bouillon

1 medium tomato, chopped

2 tbsp chopped fresh cilantro or parsley

2 tbsp toasted coconut

fresh cilantro, to garnish

1 Heat the butter in a heavy or non-stick pan and sauté the chicken with the onion for about 3 minutes.

2 Stir in the turmeric, cinnamon, rice and seasoning and sauté gently for 3 minutes.

3 Add the unsweetened yogurt, golden raisins, and chicken bouillon and mix well. Cover and simmer for 10 minutes, stirring occasionally until the rice is tender and all the bouillon has been absorbed. Add more bouillon if the mixture becomes too dry.

4 Stir in the chopped tomato and fresh cilantro or parsley.

5 Sprinkle the pilau with the toasted coconut and garnish with fresh cilantro.

cook's tip

Long-grain rice is the most widely available and the cheapest rice. Basmati, with its slender grains and aromatic flavor, is more expensive and should be used on special occasions if it is not affordable on a frequent basis. Rice, especially basmati, should be washed thoroughly under cold, running water before use.

chicken drumsticks deep-fried with herbs & spices

This dinner-party dish should ideally be cooked and served from a karahi, but if you do not have one, a deep, heavy skillet will do.

Serves 4

8 chicken drumsticks

1½ tsp fresh ginger root, finely chopped

1½ tsp fresh garlic, crushed

1 tsp salt

2 medium onions, chopped

½ large bunch fresh cilantro leaves

4–6 green chiles

2½ cups oil

4 firm tomatoes, cut into wedges

2 large green bell peppers, roughly chopped

1 Make 2–3 slashes in each piece of chicken. Rub the ginger root, garlic, and salt over the chicken pieces and set aside.

2 Place half of the onions, the cilantro leaves, and green chiles in a pestle and mortar and grind to a paste. Rub the paste over the chicken pieces.

3 Heat the oil in a karahi or large skillet. Add the remaining onions and sauté until golden brown. Remove the onions from the pan with a draining spoon and set aside.

4 Reduce the heat to medium hot and sauté the chicken pieces, in batches of about 2 at a time, until cooked through (about 5–7 minutes).

3

5 When all of the chicken pieces are cooked through, remove them from the pan, keep warm and set aside.

6 Add the tomatoes and the bell peppers to the pan and half–cook them until they are softened but still have bite.

7 Transfer the tomatoes and bell peppers to a serving plate and arrange the chicken on top. Garnish with the reserved onions.

1

2

chicken korma

Korma is a typically mild and aromatic curry. If you want to reduce the fat in this recipe, use unsweetened yogurt instead of the cream.

Serves 4-6

1 lb 10 oz chicken meat, cut into cubes

1¼ cups heavy cream

½ tsp garam masala

KORMA PASTE

2 garlic cloves

1 inch fresh ginger root, coarsely chopped

⅓ cup blanched almonds

6 tbsp chicken bouillon

1 tsp ground cardamon

4 cloves, crushed

1 tsp cinnamon

2 large onions, chopped

1 tsp coriander seeds

2 tsp ground cumin seeds

pinch cayenne

6 tbsp olive oil

salt and pepper

cilantro leaves, to garnish

rice, to serve

1 Place all the ingredients for the korma paste into a blender or food processor and blend together until a very smooth paste is formed.

2 Place the cubes of chicken in a bowl and pour over the korma paste. Stir to coat the chicken completely with the paste. Cover and chill in the refrigerator for 3 hours to allow the flavors to permeate the chicken.

3 Simmer the meat in a large pan for 25 minutes, adding a little chicken bouillon if the mixture becomes too dry.

1

2

4

4 Add the heavy cream and garam masala to the pan and simmer for a further 15 minutes. Allow the korma to stand for 10 minutes before serving. Garnish with fresh cilantro and serve with rice.

cook's tip

Garam masala is the name given to the mixture of spices commonly used as a base in curries. It can be bought ready-mixed or you can prepare your own by grinding together 1 tsp cardamon seeds, 2 tsp cloves, 2 tbsp each cumin seeds, and coriander seeds, 3 inch piece cinnamon stick, 1 tbsp black peppercorns, and 1 dried red chili.

chile coconut chicken

This tasty Thai-style dish has a classic sauce of lime, peanut, coconut, and chile. You'll find coconut cream in most stores or delicatessens.

Serves 4

²⁄₃ cup hot chicken bouillon

¹⁄₃ cup coconut cream

1 tbsp sunflower oil

8 skinless, boneless chicken thighs,
    cut into long, thin strips

1 small red chili, sliced thinly

4 scallions, sliced thinly

4 tbsp smooth or crunchy peanut butter

finely grated rind and juice of 1 lime

boiled rice, to serve

scallion flower and red chile, to garnish

2

3 Add the sliced red chile and the scallions to the pan and cook gently for a few minutes, stirring to mix all the ingredients.

4 Add the peanut butter, coconut cream, lime rind and juice, and simmer uncovered, stirring, for about 5 minutes.

5 Serve with boiled rice, garnished with a scallion flower and a red chile.

4

1 Place the chicken bouillon in a measuring pitcher and crumble the creamed coconut into the bouillon, stirring to dissolve.

2 Heat the oil in a wok or large heavy skillet and cook the chicken strips, stirring, until golden.

1

cook's tip

Serve jasmine rice with this spicy dish. It has a fragrant aroma that is well-suited to Thai-style recipes.

variation

Limes are used frequently in Thai cookery, particularly in conjunction with sweet flavors such as coconut or peanut. They are used in preference to lemons because they have a more acidic flavor which lends freshness and tartness to many dishes. If limes are unavailable, you can use lemons instead.

regal chicken with cashew nut stuffing

Most of the flavorful stuffing is cooked separately from the chicken, only a small amount being added to the neck end.

Serves 4

1 chicken, weighing about 3 lb 5 oz

1 small onion, halved

2 tbsp butter, melted

1 tsp ground turmeric

1 tsp ground ginger

½ tsp cayenne

salt and pepper

gravy, to serve

fresh cilantro, to garnish

STUFFING

2 tbsp oil

1 medium onion, finely chopped

½ medium red bell pepper, finely chopped

2 garlic cloves, finely chopped

½ cup basmati rice

1½ cups hot chicken bouillon

grated rind of ½ lemon

½ tsp ground turmeric

½ tsp ground ginger

½ tsp ground coriander

pinch cayenne pepper

½ cup salted cashew nuts

pepper

2

2

1 To make the stuffing, heat the oil in a pan, add the onion, red bell pepper, and garlic, and cook gently for 4–5 minutes. Add the rice and stir to coat in the oil. Add the bouillon, bring to a boil, then simmer for 15 minutes until all the liquid is absorbed. Transfer to a bowl and add the remaining ingredients for the stuffing. Season well with pepper.

2 Place half the stuffing in the neck end of the chicken and secure with a toothpick. Put the halved onion into the cavity of the chicken. Spoon the rest of the rice stuffing into a greased ovenproof dish and cover with foil.

3 Place the chicken in a roasting pan. Prick all over avoiding the stuffed area. Mix the butter and spices, season, then brush over the chicken.

3

4 Roast in a preheated oven, 375°F, for 1 hour, basting from time to time. Place the dish of rice stuffing in the oven and continue cooking the chicken for 30 minutes. Remove the toothpick and garnish with fresh cilantro. Serve the chicken with stuffing and gravy.

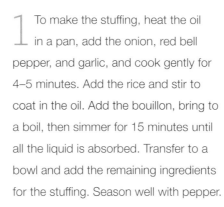

chicken tikka

For this very popular dish, small pieces of chicken are marinated in yogurt and spices for a minimum of 3 hours.

2

3

Serves 6

1 tsp fresh ginger root, finely chopped

1 tsp fresh garlic, finely chopped

½ tsp ground coriander

½ tsp ground cumin

1 tsp chili powder

3 tbsp yogurt

1 tsp salt

2 tbsp lemon juice

a few drops of red food coloring (optional)

1 tbsp tomato paste

3 lb 5 oz chicken breast

1 onion, sliced

3 tbsp oil

6 lettuce leaves

1 lemon, cut into wedges, to garnish

1 Blend together the ginger root, garlic, ground coriander, ground cumin, and chili powder in a large mixing bowl.

2 Add the yogurt, salt, lemon juice, red food coloring (if using), and the tomato paste to the spice mixture.

3 Using a sharp knife, cut the chicken into pieces. Add the chicken to the spice mixture and toss to coat well. Leave to marinate for at least 3 hours, preferably overnight.

3

4 Arrange the onion in the bottom of a heatproof dish. Carefully drizzle half of the oil over the onions.

5 Arrange the marinated chicken pieces on top of the onions and cook under a pre–heated broiler, turning once and basting with the remaining oil, for 25–30 minutes.

6 Serve on a bed of lettuce and garnish with the lemon wedges.

cook's tip

Chicken Tikka can be served with shop-bought naan breads and relish and raita (a mixture of chopped garlic and cucumber with unsweetened yogurt).

chicken with black bean sauce

This tasty chicken stir-fry is quick and easy to make and is full of fresh flavors and crunchy vegetables.

Serves 4

14 oz chicken breasts, sliced thinly

pinch of cornstarch

2 tbsp oil

1 garlic clove, finely chopped

1 tbsp black bean sauce

1 each small red and green bell pepper,
     cut into strips

1 red chile, chopped finely

1 cup mushrooms, sliced

1 onion, chopped

6 scallions, chopped

salt and pepper

fresh noodles, to serve

SEASONING

½ tsp salt

½ tsp sugar

3 tbsp chicken bouillon

1 tbsp dark soy sauce

2 tbsp beef bouillon

2 tbsp rice wine

1 tsp cornstarch, blended with a little
     rice wine

1 Put the chicken strips in a bowl. Add a pinch of salt and a pinch of cornstarch and cover with water. Leave for 30 minutes.

2 Heat 1 tbsp of the oil in a wok or deep-sided skillet and stir-fry the chicken for 4 minutes. Transfer the chicken to a warm serving dish and clean the wok or pan.

3

3 Add the remaining oil to the wok and add the garlic, black bean sauce, green and red bell peppers, chile, mushrooms, onion, and scallions. Stir-fry the vegetables for 2 minutes then return the chicken to the wok.

4 Add the seasoning, stir-fry for 3 minutes, and thicken with a little of the cornstarch paste. Serve.

1

2

cook's tip

Black bean sauce can be found in specialist shops and in many stores. Use dried noodles if you can't find fresh noodles.

chicken on crispy noodles

Blanched noodles are cooked in the wok until crisp and brown, and then topped with a shredded chicken sauce for a delightfully tasty dish.

Serves 4

8 oz skinless, boneless chicken breasts,
  shredded

1 egg white

5 tsp cornstarch

8 oz thin egg noodles

1⅔ cups vegetable oil

2½ cups chicken bouillon

2 tbsp dry sherry

2 tbsp oyster sauce

1 tbsp light soy sauce

1 tbsp hoisin sauce

1 red bell pepper, seeded and very thinly
  sliced

2 tbsp water

3 scallions, chopped

2

2

1 Mix the chicken, egg white, and
2 teaspoons of the cornstarch in a
bowl. Let stand for at least 30 minutes.

2 Blanch the noodles in boiling water
for 2 minutes, then drain thoroughly.
Heat half of the oil in a preheated wok.
Add the noodles, spreading them to
cover the base of the wok. Cook over a
low heat for about 5 minutes, until the
noodles are browned on the underside.
Flip the noodles over and brown on the
other side. Remove from the wok when
crisp and browned, place on a serving
plate, and keep warm. Drain the oil from
the wok.

3 Add 1¼ cups of the chicken bouillon
to the wok. Remove from the heat
and add the chicken, stirring well so that
it does not stick. Return to the heat and
cook for 2 minutes. Drain, discarding
the bouillon.

4 Wipe the wok with paper towels
and return to the heat. Add the
sherry, oyster sauce, soy sauce, hoisin
sauce, red bell pepper, and the
remaining chicken bouillon and bring to
a boil. Blend the remaining cornstarch
with the water to form a paste and stir it
into the mixture.

5 Return the chicken to the wok and
cook over a low heat for 2 minutes.
Place the chicken on top of the noodles
and sprinkle with scallions. Serve
immediately.

5

potato, leek & chicken pie

This pie has an attractive phyllo pie shell that has a ruffled top made with strips of the pie dough brushed with melted butter.

Serves 4

8 oz waxy potatoes, cubed

½ cup butter

1 skinned chicken breast fillet,
    about 6 oz, cubed

1 leek, sliced

5½ oz chestnut mushrooms, sliced

½ cup all–purpose flour

1¼ cups milk

1 tbsp Dijon mustard

2 tbsp chopped fresh sage

salt and pepper

8 oz phyllo pie dough, thawed if frozen

3 tbsp butter, melted

cook's tip

If the top of the pie starts to brown too quickly, cover it with foil halfway through the cooking time to allow the pie dough base to cook through without the top burning.

1 Cook the potato cubes in a pan of boiling water for 5 minutes. Drain and set aside.

2 Melt the butter in a skillet and cook the chicken cubes for 5 minutes or until browned all over.

3 Add the leek and mushrooms and cook for 3 minutes, stirring. Stir in the flour and cook for 1 minute. Gradually add the milk and bring to a boil. Add the mustard, chopped sage, and potato cubes, then leave the mixture to simmer for 10 minutes. Season to taste.

3

4

5

4 Meanwhile, line a deep pie dish with half of the sheets of phyllo pie dough. Spoon the sauce into the dish and cover with one sheet of pie dough. Brush the pie dough with butter and lay another sheet on top. Brush this sheet with butter.

5 Cut the remaining pie dough into strips and fold them on to the top of the pie to create a ruffled effect. Brush the strips with the melted butter and cook in a preheated oven, 350°F, for 45 minutes or until golden brown and crisp. Serve hot.

chicken & rice casserole

This is a spicy casserole of rice, chicken and vegetables in a soy and ginger flavored liquor. Although called a casserole, the dish only requires approximately 30 minutes cooking time.

Serves 4

⅔ cup long–grain rice

1 tbsp dry sherry

2 tbsp light soy sauce

2 tbsp dark soy sauce

2 tsp dark brown sugar

1 tsp salt

1 tsp sesame oil

2 lb skinless, boneless chicken meat, diced

3¾ cups chicken bouillon

2 open–cap mushrooms, sliced

2 oz water chestnuts, halved

3 oz broccoli flowerets

1 yellow bell pepper, sliced

4 tsp grated fresh ginger root

whole chives, to garnish

1 Cook the rice in a pan of boiling water for about 15 minutes. Drain well, rinse under cold water, and drain again thoroughly.

2 Place the sherry, soy sauces, sugar, salt, and sesame oil in a large bowl and mix together until well combined.

3 Stir the chicken into the soy mixture, turning to coat well. Leave to marinate for about 30 minutes.

4 Bring the bouillon to a boil in a saucepan or preheated wok.

5 Add the chicken with the marinade, mushrooms, water chestnuts, broccoli, bell pepper, and ginger root.

3

6

6 Stir in the rice, reduce the heat, cover, and cook for 25–30 minutes, until the chicken and vegetables are cooked through.

7 Transfer to serving plates, garnish with chives and serve.

variation

This dish would work equally well with beef or pork. Chinese dried mushrooms may be used instead of the open-cap mushrooms, if rehydrated before adding to the dish.

2

potato, chicken & banana cakes

Potato cakes are a great favorite, but are usually served plain as a side dish. In this recipe, the potatoes are combined with minced chicken and mashed banana for a fruit-flavored main course.

Serves 4

1 lb mealy potatoes, diced

8 oz ground chicken

1 large banana

2 tbsp all-purpose flour

1 tsp lemon juice

1 onion, finely chopped

2 tbsp chopped fresh sage

salt and pepper

2 tbsp butter

2 tbsp vegetable oil

⅔ cup light cream

⅔ cup chicken bouillon

fresh sage leaves, to garnish

2

3

4

1 Cook the diced potatoes in a pan of boiling water for 10 minutes until cooked through. Drain and mash the potatoes until smooth. Stir in the chicken.

2 Mash the banana and add it to the potato with the flour, lemon juice, onion, and half of the chopped sage. Season well and stir the mixture together.

3 Divide the mixture into 8 equal portions. With lightly floured hands, shape each portion into a round patty.

4 Heat the butter and oil in a skillet, add the potato cakes, and cook for 12–15 minutes or until cooked through, turning once. Remove from the skillet and keep warm.

5 Stir the cream and bouillon into the skillet with the remaining chopped sage. Cook over a low heat for 2–3 minutes.

6 Arrange the potato cakes on a serving plate, garnish with fresh sage leaves, and serve with the cream and sage sauce.

cook's tip

Do not boil the sauce once the cream has been added as it will curdle. Cook it gently over a very low heat.

crispy chicken

In this recipe, the chicken is brushed with a syrup and deep-fried until golden. It is a little time-consuming, but well worth the effort.

Serves 4

3 lb 5 oz oven–ready chicken

2 tbsp honey

2 tsp Chinese five–spice powder

2 tbsp rice wine vinegar

3¾ cups vegetable oil, for frying

chili sauce, to serve

cook's tip

If it is easier, use chicken portions instead of a whole chicken. You could also use chicken legs for this recipe, if you prefer.

1 Rinse the chicken inside and out under cold running water and pat dry with paper towels.

2 Bring a large pan of water to a boil and remove from the heat. Place the chicken in the water, cover, and set aside for 20 minutes. Remove the chicken from the water and pat dry with paper towels. Cool and leave to chill in the refrigerator overnight.

3 To make the glaze, mix the honey, Chinese five–spice powder, and rice wine vinegar.

4 Brush some of the glaze all over the chicken and return to the refrigerator for 20 minutes. Repeat this process until all of the glaze has been used up. Return the chicken to the refrigerator for at least 2 hours after the final coating.

5

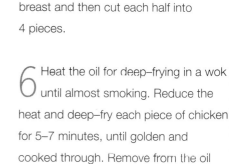

2

2

5 Using a cleaver or heavy kitchen knife, open the chicken out by splitting it through the center of the breast and then cut each half into 4 pieces.

6 Heat the oil for deep–frying in a wok until almost smoking. Reduce the heat and deep–fry each piece of chicken for 5–7 minutes, until golden and cooked through. Remove from the oil with a draining spoon and drain on absorbent paper towels.

7 Transfer to a serving dish and serve hot with chili sauce.

braised chicken

This is a delicious way to cook a whole chicken. It has a wonderful glaze, which is served as a sauce.

Serves 4

3 lb 5 oz chicken

3 tbsp vegetable oil

1 tbsp peanut oil

2 tbsp dark brown sugar

5 tbsp dark soy sauce

⅔ cup water

2 garlic cloves, finely chopped

1 small onion, chopped

1 fresh red chile, chopped

celery leaves and chives, to garnish

2

3

2

cook's tip

When caramelizing the sugar, do not turn the heat too high, otherwise it may burn.

1 Clean the chicken inside and out with damp paper towels.

2 Put the oils in a large wok, add the sugar, and heat gently until the sugar caramelizes. Stir in the soy sauce. Add the chicken and turn it in the mixture to coat thoroughly on all sides.

3 Add the water, garlic, onion, and chile. Cover and simmer, turning the chicken, for about 1 hour, or until cooked through. Test by piercing a thigh with the point of a knife—the juices run clear when the chicken is done.

4 Remove the chicken from the wok and set aside. Increase the heat and reduce the sauce in the wok until thickened. Transfer the chicken to a serving plate, garnish with celery leaves and chives, and serve with the sauce.

variation

For a spicier sauce, add 1 tbsp finely chopped fresh ginger root and 1 tbsp ground Szechuan peppercorns with the chili in step 3. If the flavor of dark soy sauce is too strong for your taste, substitute 2 tbsp dark soy sauce and 3 tbsp light soy sauce. This will result in a more delicate taste without sacrificing the attractive color of the dish.

creamy chicken & potato casserole

Small new potatoes are ideal for this recipe as they can be cooked whole. If larger potatoes are used, cut them in half or into chunks before adding them to the casserole.

Serves 4

2 tbsp vegetable oil

¼ cup butter

4 chicken portions, about 8 oz each

2 leeks, sliced

1 garlic clove, finely chopped

4 tbsp all-purpose flour

3¾ cups chicken bouillon

1¼ cups dry white wine

salt and pepper

4½ oz baby carrots, halved lengthways

4½ oz baby corn, halved lengthways

1 lb small new potatoes

1 bouquet garni

⅔ cup heavy cream

plain rice and fresh vegetables, to serve

cook's tip

Use turkey fillets instead of the chicken, if preferred, and vary the vegetables according to those you have to hand.

1

3

5

1 Heat the oil and butter in a large skillet. Cook the chicken for 10 minutes, turning until browned all over. Transfer the chicken to a casserole dish using a draining spoon.

2 Add the leek and garlic to the skillet and cook for 2–3 minutes, stirring. Stir in the flour and cook for a further 1 minute. Remove the skillet from the heat and stir in the bouillon and wine. Season well.

3 Return the pan to the heat and bring the mixture to a boil. Stir in the carrots, corn, potatoes, and bouquet garni.

4 Transfer the mixture to the casserole dish. Cover and cook in a preheated oven, 350°F, for about 1 hour.

5 Remove the casserole from the oven and stir in the cream. Return the casserole to the oven, uncovered, and cook for a further 15 minutes. Remove the bouquet garni and discard. Taste and adjust the seasoning, if necessary. Serve the casserole with plain rice or fresh vegetables such as broccoli.

five-spice chicken with onion rice

This dish has a wonderful color obtained from the turmeric, and a great spicy flavor, making it very appealing all round.

Serves 4

1 tbsp Chinese five-spice powder

2 tbsp cornstarch

12 oz boneless, skinless chicken breasts, cubed

3 tbsp peanut oil

1 onion, diced

1 cup long-grain white rice

½ tsp turmeric

2½ cups chicken bouillon

2 tbsp snipped fresh chives

cook's tip

Be careful when using turmeric as it can stain the hands and clothes a distinctive shade of yellow.

1

2   5

1 Place the Chinese five-spice powder and cornstarch in a large bowl. Add the chicken pieces and toss to coat all over.

2 Heat 2 tablespoons of the peanut oil in a large preheated wok. Add the chicken pieces to the wok and stir-fry for 5 minutes. Using a draining spoon, remove the chicken and set aside.

3 Add the remaining peanut oil to the wok.

4 Add the onion to the wok and stir-fry for 1 minute.

5 Add the rice, turmeric, and chicken bouillon to the wok and bring to a boil.

6 Return the chicken pieces to the wok, reduce the heat, and leave to simmer for 10 minutes, or until the liquid has been absorbed and the rice is tender.

7 Add the chives, stir to mix, and serve hot.

index